MW00974170

Composing Your Own
Financial Symphony

FIVE CONCERNS FACING RETIREES TODAY AND FOUR
SIMPLE STRATEGIES TO ADDRESS THEM

Mark Lloyd

The Lloyd Group
SUWANEE, GEORGIA

Copyright © 2018 by Mark Lloyd.

All rights reserved. No part of this publication may be reproduced, distributed or transmitted in any form or by any means, including photocopying, recording, or other electronic or mechanical methods, without the prior written permission of the publisher, except in the case of brief quotations embodied in critical reviews and certain other noncommercial uses permitted by copyright law. For permission requests, write to the publisher at the address below.

Mark Lloyd/The Lloyd Group
3575 Lawrenceville Suwanee Road
Suwanee, GA 30024
www.thelloydgroupinc.com

Book layout ©2013 BookDesignTemplates.com

Composing Your Own Financial Symphony/ Mark Lloyd. —1st ed.

ISBN-978-1720563426

The Lloyd Group is an independent financial services firm that helps individuals create retirement strategies using a variety of investment and insurance products to custom suit their needs and objectives. Investment advisory services offered only by duly registered individuals through Lloyd Advisory Services.

The contents of this book are provided for informational purposes only and are not intended to serve as the basis for any financial decisions. Any tax, legal or estate planning information is general in nature. It should not be construed as legal or tax advice. Always consult an attorney or tax professional regarding the applicability of this information to your unique situation.

Information presented is believed to be factual and up-to-date, but we do not guarantee its accuracy and it should not be regarded as a complete analysis of the subjects discussed. All expressions of opinion are those of the author as of the date of publication and are subject to change. Content should not be construed as personalized investment advice nor should it be interpreted as an offer to buy or sell any securities mentioned. A financial advisor should be consulted before implementing any of the strategies presented.

Investing involves risk, including the potential loss of principal. No investment strategy can guarantee a profit or protect against loss in periods of declining values. Any references to protection benefits or guaranteed/lifetime income streams generally refer to fixed insurance products, never securities or investment products. Insurance and annuity product guarantees are backed by the financial strength and claims-paying ability of the issuing insurance company.

Contents

To the next generation...

Foreword
by Don Yaeger

I've been blessed over the course of a career to work with some of the greatest coaches of all time. I've written books or articles with everyone from legendary UCLA coach John Wooden to Tennessee's Pat Summitt; Alabama's Nick Saban to Duke's Mike Krzyzewski. Finding the best coach is, without question, the differentiator in anyone's pursuit of great things.

In the study of those great coaches, a number of similarities stand out. Discipline. Passion. Great communicators. But the one trait that is an absolute: The BEST coaches are flexible; they don't do the same thing no matter who they're working with. They adjust the way they teach and what they teach based on the players they have on their roster. Their game plan changes depending on who they are charged with leading.

When an athlete finds the right coach, that coach helps them blossom by building a plan that takes advantage of where they are at the moment and what they can become with development.

That lesson has extended for me over the years watching how great coaching impacts public speakers, business leaders and ... people building their long-term financial health.

In this book, Mark coaches you! He explains how to build a financial road map and how that road map will dictate the way you will find your OWN level of success. Lloyd breaks down the industry in ways that even simple sports writers like myself can understand.

At the end, he brings you alongside with the right coaching. In this book, Mark encourages you to find YOUR coach and he spells out for you the questions you should be asking to ensure you find that coach. I dog-eared those pages because I found them so valuable.

One of my favorite phrases is, "Greatness is available to all of us who are willing to do the common things uncommonly well." Composing Your Own Financial Symphony is the perfect guide to help make this process work for you. It is a collection of common things you can do uncommonly well.

I trust the information Mark provides in this book. And I believe you will find much here that will allow you to grow and be successful.

Be GREAT,

Don Yaeger

Nine-time New York Times best-selling author, "Great Teams: 16 Things High-Performing Organizations Do Differently"

Preface

When I was a young child, my mother led Bible studies and taught Sunday school in our church. As I write this book, she is almost 90 years old, and often says how much she misses teaching.

What is it they say? The acorn doesn't fall far from the tree? Maybe that explains why I love to share what I have learned about money with my clients and people I meet from our nationally-aired radio program, "The Financial Symphony" and TV show of the same name. I also enjoy meeting people from all walks of life while conducting seminars. Growing up, my mother was grooming me, and I didn't even know it.

Looking back, it's the time we spend growing up that molds us into who we are going to be and what we are going to become. We were a family that helped people. It was just what we did. So, it made sense when I started my financial advisory practice, I envisioned helping people forge their financial futures would be job No. 1. I was right. It was and still is.

Frankly, I am concerned about the financial future of many Americans today. I was born Aug. 2, 1961. That officially qualifies me as a "baby boomer" (people born from 1946 to 1964). Fewer and fewer people of my generation will benefit from the guaranteed income of a pension. Pensions are an endangered species and have almost vanished from the economic scene. Forget living off Social Security. It's not enough to cover day-to-day living expenses for those of my generation, and the very existence of Social Security is threatened for future generations. Generation

X (children of baby boomers), and millennials (children of Gen-Xers) will be forced to either save diligently or live off the government.

Information Overload

We live in an age of instancy — instant coffee, instant tea, instant news. Television and the internet has whittled away our tolerance for delay. If a catastrophe happens halfway around the globe, we expect (and usually receive) video of it within the hour. This phenomenon has been called "The Information Age." The 24-hour news cycles and the availability of millions of websites accessible with the touch of a button have given us such an over-abundance of knowledge and information. The problem is, it can sometimes be overwhelming.

When it comes to investing, for example, we are deluged with advice. I was in an airport recently and stopped by a newsstand to pick up a magazine to read on the plane. There was an entire wall of magazines to choose from, covering virtually every interest imaginable. Sports, music, food, hobbies, vacation spots, home design. The number of topics seemed endless.

I didn't count them, but there was an entire section of the wall dedicated to financial advice. Some names I recognized. There was "Kiplinger," "Barron's," and "Money Magazine." But there were many others I had never heard of. All these magazines were competing for attention with eye-catching headlines offering investing advice in flashy, bold type:

- *"Four Undervalued Stocks in an Overpriced Market"*
- *"It's Getting Ugly Out There: Dow Drops 98 Points as Tech, Biotech Tumble"*
- *"Stocks Rally: Dow Up Triple Digits"*
- *"Top 100 Hedge Funds"*
- *"12 Consumer Stocks with Nice Payouts"*

That's just a sampling. I thought to myself, "It is no wonder ordinary investors are so confused these days. All they want to do is know how to prudently invest their savings, but when they look for answers, they have so many people yelling advice to them from the sidelines, they throw up their hands in frustration, not knowing what to do or whom to listen to."

It seems that everyone wants to offer investment advice these days. From good old Uncle Bob at family reunions telling you about the next Google or Apple to the guy at the office who hangs around the water cooler whispering to you about the hot stock tip he heard about from a friend who told him not to tell. That's not to mention the plethora of financial channels on TV with bickering talking heads each pushing a different investing philosophy. It's like drinking from a fire hydrant — it's overwhelming, and it can be hazardous to your wealth!

A Case in Point

As I write this book, I have enjoyed over 25 years of helping families plan for their financial futures. In that time, I have come across certain individuals who have made a lasting impact on my life. Their stories usually involve instances where they were lost and needed help. Not all of them have happy endings, I'm afraid.

In early 2002, I met a sweet lady who had attended one of my educational classes and introduced herself to me. To protect her privacy, we will call her Mary. Mary set an appointment with me for a free consultation. On her first visit, she brought with her a brown expanding file folder containing all her financial statements. She told me her husband had died just a little over a year ago, and the balance in her investment accounts was around $290,000. Besides some "rainy-day money" at the bank, this represented her entire nest egg.

The shocking part of her story was what she told me after laying out her current financial picture.

"Mark, this account used to contain over a million dollars," said the 78-year-old widow. "I lost it in the stock market crash."

She was referring to the 2000 market crash when the tech bubble burst.

Just before he died, her husband told her, "Honey, whatever you do, don't sell the stocks." It was a portfolio that contained several high-risk tech stocks.

Naturally, Mary was torn. She wanted to honor her husband's death-bed wishes, but she also realized her husband had no idea the market would crash when he had spoken those words to her. He had thought those dot-com stocks would keep right on increasing in value, and make her a wealthy woman after his passing. But the market crash had changed everything. She wondered what her husband would want her to do. She needed advice desperately.

Mary went to her stockbroker.

"Your husband knew what he was talking about," her stockbroker told her. "Just hold on. It will come back. It always comes back."

In one sense, her stockbroker was right. Historically, the stock market has always rebounded after a severe downturn. But Mary was 78 years old! Did her stockbroker think it was OK for a 78-year-old widow, conservative by nature, to be so heavily invested in high-risk stocks? Didn't he realize it would take several years — time Mary didn't have — for the stocks to bounce back? What about her income in the meantime? If he had asked about that, he would have seen she had a problem. When her husband had died, she lost a Social Security check she depended upon to make ends meet. She had no pension. Mary needed income and the stocks remaining in the portfolio returned very low interest and produced little in the way of dividends.

If her stockbroker had asked her about long-term care insurance, he would have discovered she had none. What would happen to Mary if her health failed, and she needed long-term care in an assisted living facility or a nursing home? Her investment accounts would evaporate in a nursing home spend-down, and she would end up penniless and a ward of the state.

Where was the disconnect? Her broker was treating her like a long-term investor. The old, "don't worry, it will come back" line might have worked for a 40-something investor with a job and time on her hands, but not for someone Mary's age.

You must excuse me for a few minutes while I take something to settle my stomach. Just reliving this story and putting it down on paper for you has made me a bit nauseated.

Five Major Retirement Concerns

At the supermarket where I buy groceries, there is a rack of free magazines. Most of them are apartment finders, others are put there by real estate companies and contain pictures of houses for sale. I usually pass it by because I am not in the market for either. But recently a new one caught my eye. "Senior Living," read the title splashed across the glossy cover that displayed a photograph of a man and a woman on the beach in casual attire. The couple appeared to be in their 60s. The woman had salt-and-pepper hair tossed slightly back by a gentle sea breeze. She squinted out at the gentle surf while her husband, whose hair was solid silver, crouched down to pet their golden retriever. The people, the weather — heck, even the dog — seemed to be perfect! They had not a care in the world!

The magazine's art department had captured the essence of what most people want their retirement to be. Happy, carefree "golden years" when they finally have time to do whatever they want with their lives.

You probably won't find any magazines devoted to senior living with pictures of sad-faced people at a kitchen counter, worrying about how they are going to make it through the month, or where the money is going to come from for their everyday expenses. From a marketing standpoint, that would go over like ants at a picnic, wouldn't it?

But the unvarnished truth is this: The financial landscape of retirement can be treacherous if you don't know where you are and where you are going. It is not unfair to compare the retirement adventure to a journey through dangerous territory, rife with potential wrong turns. To avoid losing your way, you need a good map and reliable, professional guidance — a sampling of which I hope you will see presented in the following pages.

I thank you for buying this book, dear reader. But if you bought it expecting to find a get-rich-quick formula, or directions to Easy Street via hot stock tips, you will be disappointed (please see me personally and I will see to it you get a refund).

Please also know the paperweight on my desk is only that. It is not a crystal ball. Trying to time the stock market is a fool's errand. Those who try to do it fail, and any who claim they can time the market are dribbling water on your head and telling you it's raining. It's simply not possible. But that still doesn't stop some mutual fund managers and other Wall Street types from claiming they have such extrasensory powers. They, of course, don't. No one does.

What you will find in this book are practical, workable solutions to a few of the everyday problems faced by baby boomers who have retired or are approaching retirement. This book will also explore five major retirement concerns. I will also share four simple strategies that will show you how to save and invest prudently to prepare for a carefree life in your sunset years — just the kind you expect and deserve. Although I've broken most of the "pieces" of retirement income strategies down into separate parts, it's important to keep in mind the most effective strategy is one in which all parts are coordinated and working together. That's when you get a true Financial Symphony.

CHAPTER ONE

"That Costs WHAT?!?"

A man, whom we will call Jack, came into my office a couple of years ago. He had prepared a budget for me to review. He had a modest nest egg of $800,000 — money he had saved through his 401(k) and some IRA rollovers from previous jobs. He had plans to start receiving his Social Security when he reached age 66. He did not have a pension, so he knew he would have to supplement his Social Security with income from his $800,000 retirement account. He had established a budget of $5,000 per month. Working with those figures, Jack calculated if he could get just the modest return of 5 percent from his investment account, he would have enough money to live on for another 22 years. What Jack didn't factor into the equation was *inflation.*

In a 2013 study, financial research organization Morningstar, using very well-known professors of finance Michael Finke from Texas Tech University and Wade Pfau from the American College, projected in their white paper that inflation could be 3.14 percent for the next 30 years. The 100-year average from the CPI

(Consumer Price Index) is 3.31 percent. Using these numbers, Jack would run out of money in 15 years.[1]

In a Morningstar Special Report published in 2011, one analyst put it this way: "Compounded over many years, inflation can actually be an enormous swing factor. Accounting for a normal inflation rate of 3.5 percent can more than double the amount that a 50-year-old investor needs to sock away for retirement."[2]

As I write this, inflation has been relatively low in recent years. Perhaps that is why Jack just didn't think about inflation as being a factor when he was doing his calculations. But this blindness to the potential effects of inflation appears epidemic among stockbrokers, judging from some of the analysis I have seen through the years.

For years, our firm has used something we call our "Financial Road Map" for clients to factor inflation into their income plan. We project it out until their age 100. OK, that may be a little optimistic. Do we believe everyone is going to live to be 100? Of course not. But it is better to always be prepared. My oldest client to date is 97. During one of her annual reviews, she said, "I don't know how much longer I will be here."

"I do," I told her. "I want to have a party for you to celebrate your 100th birthday."

The older we get, the more we can see the slow-but-continuous effect of inflation on our purchasing power. This woman can tell some interesting stories about what things cost when she was younger.

---

[1] Darla Mercado. InvestmentNews. Feb. 7, 2013. "The magic withdrawal number in a low-interest rate retirement? You'll be surprised." http://www.investment-news.com/article/20130207/FREE/130209947/the-magic-withdrawal-number-in-a-low-interest-rate-retirement-youll.

[2] Morningstar. July 23, 2011. "Morningstar's Inflation Report." http://news.morningstar.com/articlenet/article.aspx?id=386275.

I play a little game at my educational workshops. I will ask the audience, "How many of you can tell me what a gallon of gasoline cost back in 1970?"

I get all kinds of answers.

"62 cents a gallon."

"59 cents a gallon."

"20 cents a gallon."

The actual cost of a gallon of gasoline in 1970 was around 27 cents a gallon, according to the U.S. Department of Energy.[3]

Also, back in those days, there was no self-service. When you pulled into the gas station, a uniformed attendant would sprint to your car and pump the gas for you, check your oil, clean your windshield and do it all with a smile. The local gas station where I grew up was just down the street from my house. I can still recall when we bought gas there, we received something called S&H green stamps. My job was to lick them and paste the into a book. Every time my parents filled up the family automobile, they received a page of stamps. If you collected enough stamps, you were rewarded with an appliance of your choice, like a blender or a toaster. My point is, your 27 cents went a long way back in 1970.

As I write this, we are looking at somewhere between $2.20 and $2.50 per gallon for a gallon of gasoline, depending on what grade of gasoline you use. It wasn't too long ago that some gas stations were charging $5.00 a gallon for gas.

Here's another example. What was the average cost of a new home in 1973? Folks have guessed anywhere from $30,000 to $80,000. The answer is $32,000. According to U.S. Census Bureau and U.S. Department of Housing and Urban Development

---

[3] Energy.gov. March 7, 2016. "Fact #915: March 7, 2016 Average Historical Annual Gasoline Pump Price, 1929-2015." https://energy.gov/eere/vehicles/fact-915-march-7-2016-average-historical-annual-gasoline-pump-price-1929-2015.

figures released in December of 2017, the average cost of a new home has now risen to $377,100.[4]

The cost of items found at McDonalds restaurants is a good barometer of inflation. When the chain first began operating in 1955, a standard, single-patty burger sold for 15 cents. A colleague of mine showed me an old menu from McDonald's the other day with prices from the early 1970s. A quarter-pounder with cheese cost 70 cents, a Big Mac was 65 cents, and their regular hamburger cost 28 cents. You could buy a cup of coffee for 15 cents (and you didn't have to be a senior citizen to get it). In

---

[4] U.S. Census Bureau and U.S. Department of Housing and Urban Development. Dec. 22, 2017. "Monthly New Residential Sales, November 2017." https://www.census.gov/construction/nrs/pdf/newressales.pdf.

those days, I could have taken $5 and bought just about everything on this menu (and really blow my diet). Nowadays, $5 will barely pay for a kid's meal for one of my grandchildren.

McDonald's menu from the early 1970s.

McDonald's menu from the mid-1950s.

Inflation Is Unpredictable

Think of inflation as a slow-moving river, and you are in a canoe paddling upstream. You are paddling toward a goal of financial independence, and you are making progress. But your money is flowing the other way.

Another apt metaphor is beach erosion. You don't notice it day-by-day, but one day you happen to notice your little cottage by the sea is much closer to the water than it was the year before. It's like that with our wealth. Daily, inflation is imperceptible, but over time it can drastically diminish your wealth. We simply *must* factor inflation into any viable retirement plan.

As inflation rises, your dollar buys a smaller percentage of whatever it is you are buying. For example, if the inflation rate is 2 percent, then a $1 pack of gum will cost $1.02 in a year.

When I draw up financial plans for clients, I usually allow for a 3.14 percent inflation rate. The central banks of most countries these days try to maintain an inflation rate of 2–3 percent per year. From time to time, however, not even the maneuverings of the largest banks in the world can prevent runaway inflation, or hyperinflation, as it is sometimes called. Regular inflation is a protracted process. It is usually so gradual you don't even notice it. *Hyperinflation,* on the other hand, comes on fast and is felt by every sector of the economy right away.

Have you ever seen those nature shows where scientists shoot a large wild animal, like a grizzly bear, for instance, with a sedative dart so they can examine and tag it for research? Those scenes always make me nervous. I keep thinking, "What happens if that dozing grizzly wakes up and begins tossing those people around like rag dolls?"

Inflation is like that animal. For the moment, it is under sedation. But Americans old enough to remember the late 1970s saw that sleeping bear come to life and go on a rampage for a few years. It happened during the days of miniskirts, disco, polyester suits and Jimmy Carter in the White House.

Hyperinflation

When President Richard M. Nixon was sworn in on Jan. 20, 1969 as the nation's 37th president, he had inherited a recession from his predecessor, Lyndon B. Johnson. Johnson had been burning the fiscal candle at both ends. His "Great Society" program and the Vietnam War were simultaneously draining the treasury. Nixon knew that to win the 1972 election, he could not halt the social initiatives, at least not until after the election. To quell the natural economic forces at work, Nixon imposed wage and price controls in 1971. But this was just a temporary barrier, and inflation pressure continued to build. Once the controls were lifted, wages and prices rose rapidly. It was also during the Nixon administration that the link connecting American currency to gold was severed. This led to the devaluation of the American dollar and fueled the fires of inflation even more.

William Greider, in his book "Secrets of the Temple: How the Federal Reserve Runs the Country," quotes Nixon as saying: "We'll take inflation if necessary, but we can't take unemployment." Eventually, the nation had both in abundance. When Nixon won reelection in a landslide in 1972, inflation was in the low single digits. When Nixon resigned, a casualty of the Watergate investigation, he left the mess to his lame-duck vice presidential successor, Gerald R. Ford. In January 1973, the inflation rate was an acceptable 3.6 percent. By January 1974, it was at 9.4 percent, and had surged to 12 percent by the fall of that year.

Things turned comical when President Ford declared inflation "Public Enemy No. 1" before Congress on Oct. 8, 1974. In a speech entitled "Whip Inflation Now," he revealed the "WIN" button to boost support for a series of public and private steps intended to affect supply and demand and bring inflation under control. The "WIN" buttons accomplished little and became grist for comedians. Skeptics even began wearing the buttons upside down, explaining that "NIM" stood for "No Immediate Miracles," or "Nonstop Inflation Merry-go-round," or "Need Immediate Money."

This lapel button was popular in the 1980s,
but it did little to win the battle against inflation.

By the time James Earl Carter occupied the White House as the 39th president, the still-raging inflation rate would peak at 14.76 percent in March 1980.

People who saved money at banks during those days had the illusion of good times. Sure, their CDs and money market accounts grew by double-digits, but they were paying twice as much for groceries and gas as they had been five years ago. Those who had to borrow money to buy a car or a house found the payments unaffordable, so they didn't buy. The building boom stopped dead in its tracks in 1979. Entire subdivisions of homes, many built on speculation, stayed vacant for years. Ironically, as things turned out, the cure for hyperinflation was the recession the inflation had spawned.[5, 6]

Like a sailing vessel with a heavy keel, the economy will usually right itself if left alone.

Could Hyperinflation Happen Again?

As I write this, inflation seems content to rock along at just under 3 percent or so. But what about hyperinflation. Will we ever see a repeat of the 1970s? Some doomsayers warn of a return to double-digit inflation through skyrocketing energy prices. But they are speculating. What is more likely is the steady, erosion-type inflation will be with us for the foreseeable future. But even at that slow pace, we will experience an erosion of wealth that, unless you plan for it, can be like financial death by a thousand cuts.

Effect of Inflation on Income Requirements

To demonstrate how inflation pinches the retiree, consider the effect inflation would have on income requirements in three different scenarios. To make the math easy, suppose you needed to supplement your Social Security by $1,000 per month. How big would your nest egg have to be, earning 7 percent interest, if you lived 20 years in retirement? How about if you lived 30 years in retirement? Now figure in 3 percent inflation. How does that affect the picture?

---

[5] Gregory Bresiger. Investopedia. "The Great Inflation of the 1970s." https://www.investopedia.com/articles/economics/09/1970s-great-inflation.asp.

[6] William Greider. "Secrets of the Temple: How the Federal Reserve Runs the Country." Simon & Schuster, Jan. 15, 1989.

- If you live *20 years* in retirement, with no inflation, you would need a nest egg of *$129,734* earning 7% interest to produce an income of $1,000 per month income.
- With 3% inflation, if you live *20 years* in retirement, you would need a nest egg of *$163,007* earning 7% interest to produce a $1,000 per month income.
- If you live *30 years* in retirement with 3% inflation, you would need a nest egg of *$195,343* earning 7% interest to produce $1,000 per month income.

According to research performed by the Society of Actuaries (SOA), only 72 percent of pre-retirees, and 55 percent of retirees have calculated the effects of inflation on their retirement plan. Ten years into their retirement, however, they will be spending $13 to buy what $10 buys today. In 20 years, they will be spending $18 to buy what $10 will buy today.[7]

So, what are some ways to take inflation into account when planning for retirement?

- You could delay your Social Security, if possible, to age 70. Doing so, experts suggest, will give you the highest possible inflation-adjusted, guaranteed stream of income from Social Security. Depending on your age, you could increase your annual benefit up to 8% per year.
- Consider investing in an immediate income annuity with an inflation rider. Income annuities are insurance contracts purchased with a single lump sum that offer immediate income payments (usually monthly) for a specified period or for the annuitant's lifetime.
- Ask your advisor about fixed index annuities with income riders with inflation protection.

---

[7] Society of Actuaries. March 2, 2011. "Society of Actuaries' Risk Report Highlights Impact of Inflation on Retirement Planning." https://benefitslink.com/cgi-bin/pr/index.cgi?rm=press_release&id=45493.

- Put the following hard question to your financial advisor: "If I want to retire at age 65 (or whatever year you choose), how much income will I need, adjusted for inflation, and how much will I have to have saved to accomplish that?" Computer software has become available in the last few years to nail down the answer to the dollar.

When making retirement plans, there is no way to cover all possible scenarios or deal with all possible contingencies, but it is only prudent to build into our strategy the extra money we will probably need to at least compensate for the standard 3 percent inflation we know we can expect. If that requires living on a budget now so we will not have to scrimp later, then the sooner we know, the better we can adjust. If it means working a bit longer so we can hit our "magic number" in retirement, it would be prudent to do so.

By the way, those "WIN" buttons that were ridiculed back in the 1980s actually did whip inflation, in a way. Once worth 10 cents, they are now collectors' items you can buy on eBay for around $5.

One last thought on inflation: if you are a nervous investor and you have opted to have your retirement in cash or low-interest deposits because you're scared of any risk, you may be still losing. You could be losing buying power if your rate of return is less than inflation. The good news is there are choices out there to consider in the investment universe to receive a higher rate of return with either no risk of principle in the stock market or some with low risk in the market. We will discuss these later in the book.

Action Item:

Have an income plan (Financial Road Map) prepared to factor in inflation for the future.

CHAPTER TWO

No Big Roller Coasters
in Retirement

J ust west of Atlanta, the closest big city to where I work and live, is Six Flags Over Georgia — a sprawling amusement park that attracts people from all over the eastern United States. The park is home to "Batman: The Ride," a roller coaster that is not for the faint of heart. I have never been on this monster, and have no intention of riding it. I grew up in Wilmington, Delaware, and I remember going to the State Fair in Harrington one year where I rode a rickety, no-name roller coaster. That was child's play compared to the Six Flags ride. According to the promotional material published by the theme park, "Batman" riders are lifted 100 feet into the air, then sent hurtling through twists and turns, up and down, at 50 miles per hour, with their heads spinning and their feet dangling into space. The days when I thought being tossed around in such a manner was in any way fun are long gone. In fact, the older I get, the less inclined I am to take physical chances of any kind.

It is a little like that with investing, isn't it? When we are young, both our portfolios and our emotional makeup can absorb and tolerate the ups and downs of a volatile and unpredictable stock market. Big market downturn? No problem. We didn't have too much in it anyway. Besides, it will come back around eventually, right?

Then, as we age and have more at stake, we are less inclined to accept risk. This is especially true (and understandably so) as we near retirement. Financial thrill rides are chilling and uncomfortable; they make us lose sleep. If we are in retirement, we are working with nonrenewable resources and simply don't have time to wait for the market to rebound from a big downturn.

In the past, some retirees may have kept their retirement accounts in risky investments because they knew of no alternatives. Some still do that. Consequently, when the market declines, they feel it necessary to stop taking income. This restricts their lifestyle and adds to their anxiety.

Risk Is Not Our Enemy

Let me say right off the bat that risk is not necessarily our enemy. It is volatility that drives the market higher. You may compare it to gardening. By no means do I have a green thumb. But my father used to have a garden when I was a child. My job was to work in the garden. I would plow it, till it with a hoe, extract weeds from it and help pick the produce. That was the extent of my gardening experience. I can still remember him trimming back our shrubs and plants so that they would come back the next year fuller and bigger than ever.

That is how the stock market works. When there is a dip in the market, that creates a buying opportunity for savvy investors. Many an investor has made a pot of money after a market crash or correction. So, what's the problem? Most investors are not psychologically wired to see a downturn in the market as opportunity. Their emotions get in the way. As soon as they see their balance drop, they immediately begin to focus on the money they have lost. Horror begins to set in, especially if they have a significant portion of their life's savings invested.

"I will never be able to retire," they may say to themselves as they sleeplessly pace the floor at night.

Believe me, I get it. Nothing can be more frightening to someone entering what I call the "red zone" of retirement (within five years) as seeing all they have worked put in jeopardy. When this occurs, it is usually because the investor had way more at risk than what was recommended for his or her time horizon.

What is a time horizon? One of our staffers broke it down this way: "If you are spending your retirement, you need to be classified as conservative or low-risk. That would be a time horizon of now to three years of an investment cycle."

A *moderate* time horizon would be a full market cycle of three to five years. That's also called a *balanced portfolio*.

A *growth* time horizon could be six to nine years, and an aggressive could be 10 or more years. Drawing income from a growth or an aggressive portfolio is not recommended due to the volatility of the portfolio. The worst thing you could do is sell shares to produce a monthly check while the market is dropping. You would have to sell more shares to create the amount you need, and that would accelerate running out of money.

Retirement Red Zone

When you are retired or within five or 10 years of retirement, your focus should shift. You have come this far and hopefully have accumulated a measure of wealth. Your focus should now be how to preserve that wealth while you continue to accumulate to cover inflation and plan for higher taxation. Football fans can relate to the analogy of the "Retirement Red Zone."

Imagine you are the quarterback of your team. You have played well to this point. You have moved your team all the way to the opposing team's 20-yard line. That means the end zone is within sight. You wouldn't throw a long pass at this point, would you? Why not? Because the ball would likely land somewhere in the stands. You would throw short passes, or perhaps even hand the ball off to the running back to get those last 20 yards. When you handle the ball, your fingers would grip just a little tighter and you would hug the ball just a little closer to your body. You've come this far. This is no time to fumble and turn the ball over.

Similarly, when you are in the "Retirement Red Zone," you look at your portfolio differently. You are more conservative. A risky play could result in a turnover at the worst possible moment when your retirement goal is so close.

Ron and Sue

I met a couple with quite a story to tell. We will call them Ron and Sue. They had 85 percent of their portfolio in equities (stocks). The year was 2007 and they had just retired. The market had been steadily rising for the last five years, and they saw no problem whatsoever in spending $4,000 per month from their accounts. Then 2008 happened. They still needed the $4,000 per month to maintain their lifestyle, and the market was sinking like the Titanic. Unfortunately, Ron had to find work again and take a job with low pay just to make ends meet. All that could have been avoided had he recognized just how much risk (downside volatility) they had taken on.

When you are in the Retirement Red Zone, it is critical to have your portfolio stress-tested to see how much risk you have. Nobel Laureate Harry Markowitz, from the University of Chicago, won his Nobel Prize by figuring out how to measure risk in a portfolio. He has been called the "founder of the Modern Portfolio Theory" for his work in risk management. It was his contention that investors should view a portfolio invested in equities through the "lens of statistics," and that a portfolio's rate of return should be gauged in the light of its "expected value and standard deviation."

Standard deviation is, simply put, the measuring stick for risk.

For example, we know if you go back 40 years, large cap stocks have a standard deviation of 18. We know long-term government bonds have a standard deviation of 12 for that same period. Sue and Ron had a standard deviation of 19. I know that may be getting a little technical, but think of it this way. What was the biggest, fastest roller coaster you ever rode as a kid? Did you climb onto one that caused you to grip the bar so tight that it gave you white knuckles? Well, that's a standard deviation of 19. The kiddie roller coaster — that's a standard deviation of six or maybe 10. Conservative to moderate. If prudently diversified, investors might be able stay in the six to 10 range and have all the income they need, with low to moderate volatility, and still be able to sleep at night in retirement.

Action Item:

Have a stress test performed to see what your standard deviation, or your risk number, is.

CHAPTER THREE

The "Tax Time Bomb"

W e live in a tax-on-tax society.

Not only do we pay federal income taxes, but most of us pay state income tax, city tax, sales tax, FICA tax, Medicare tax, capital gains tax, possibly probate tax, possibly an estate tax, a Medicare surtax for singles with $200,000 in adjusted gross income, and a Medicare surtax for couples earning $250,000. Did I leave anything out?

Would it surprise you to learn the average American works for 114 days of the year just to pay their taxes?

According to the Tax Foundation, a Washington, D.C. think-tank organization that collects data and publishes research on national and state tax policies, "Tax Freedom Day®" in 2016 was April 24. That's the day when you stop working for the government and *finally* get to pocket your money.

Scott Greenberg, senior analyst with the Center for Federal Tax Policy at the Tax Foundation, said: "Tax Freedom Day® is the day when the nation as a whole has earned enough money to pay its total tax bill for the year. Tax Freedom Day takes all federal, state and local taxes and divides them by the nation's income."

Greenberg estimated in 2016, Americans would pay $3.34 trillion in federal taxes and $1.64 trillion in state and local taxes, for a total tax bill of $4.99 trillion, or 31 percent of national income."[8]

Consider this, too. Taxes don't go away at retirement. For most folks, at 70 ½, the Internal Revenue Service mandates we take distributions from our traditional IRAs and other qualified, or tax-deferred accounts. We call that a required minimum distribution, or an RMD. Uncle Sam is not stupid. He allows us to defer taxes on these accounts until they grow nice and plump with interest garnered over the years. That's when he takes his cut. But what if you don't need the money? Doesn't matter. The "R" in RMD, remember, stands for *required.* If you fail to take your distribution, you can be penalized up to 50 percent. Even if you don't need the income, you must pay tax on the distribution.

Pay Tax on the Seed or Harvest?

Think of taxation on qualified accounts this way: Suppose you are a farmer, and you stroll into the local feed and seed store to

---

[8] Scott Greenberg. April 6, 2016. "Tax Freedom Day 2016 is April 4." https://taxfoundation.org/tax-freedom-day-2016-april-24/.

purchase your seed for this year's planting season. After making your selection, you proceed to the counter to pay. There, you are greeted by a man dressed up like Uncle Sam — red, white and blue top hat, waist coat, and a gray goatee.

"You know you have to pay taxes on that," said Uncle Sam pointing at the bags of seed.

"Of course!" you respond.

Uncle Sam says, "I'll make you a deal, Pal. You can pay me taxes now on the seed and be done with it, or you can skip the taxes on the seed, go ahead and plant it, and just pay me taxes on the value of the harvest when it comes in."

Would you take that deal? Probably not. But millions of Americans take that deal every year when they participate in 401(k)s, 403(b)s, traditional IRAs and similar retirement programs. I know, the premise is your taxes will be lower in retirement. Maybe so, maybe not!

I have a client by the name of Tom (not his real name), who had just enjoyed his 70th birthday. Tom is a relatively new client who owns a chain of retail stores. He has over $1.5 million in a traditional IRA. I explained to Tom that he would need to begin taking RMDs when he turned 70 ½, and the total of his first withdrawal would be around $57,000. The look on his face was one of surprise and consternation.

"Ouch, that hurts," he said. "I have enough money coming in. I don't want to withdraw any more!"

Sorry, Tom. Wrong answer.

If I had met Tom earlier, we could have started converting some of his IRAs to Roth IRAs. That would have created a taxable event, true, but, if structured properly, at 70 ½ he wouldn't have been required to take out RMDs on his Roth IRA.

What makes the tax bite even worse for individuals like Tom is when his children inherit his IRA, they will have to treat it as taxable income according to their current tax bracket. Double ouch!

Fortunately, spouses can inherit an IRA and implement a spousal rollover, thus avoiding unnecessary taxation. But if the children inherit it, no such luck. There are some strategies we can use to spread the tax liability over the lifetime of his children — an inheriting child (or grandchild!) can be named as a beneficiary of the IRA and then the RMDs (and thus the accompanying taxes) will be based on the longer life expectancy of the new beneficiary.

Some mistakenly think a fat retirement account full of tax-deferred dollars equates to wealth and a secure income in retirement. Instead, what they may have is a hefty tax liability. In my work, I often find myself in the position of the bearer of bad news. I must explain to individuals that their retirement income projections don't hold up under the math test, because they have not factored taxes into the equation.

As you can see, taxes while we are living, as well as taxes at death, are a big deal. Work with an advisor who can educate you on what you can do to diffuse tax time bombs. Strategies exist that can help you minimize taxes while you are working, after you retire, and reduce the potential taxes you may be passing to your heirs. The schedule A of your 1040 can be our friend *if we have a plan.*

Action Item:

Every individual's tax liability is different. Frequent reviews are necessary to learn your options to reduce taxes while you are living, and know how to minimize taxes your family may incur when you die.

CHAPTER FOUR

Health Care Expenses — the Unknown Dilemma

What will health care in our country look like in the future? And how much will health insurance cost us in the future? That's the million-dollar question.

It was hoped that the Affordable Care Act enacted by the 111th U.S. Congress and signed into law by President Barack Obama on March 23, 2010, was going to greatly reduce premiums. And, for some with subsidies, it has. Others, however, have seen their premiums continue to increase.

So, if we are planning on retiring before reaching age 65 and Medicare eligibility, we must figure possible, if not probable, rate hikes into our retirement plan.

The good news is, when we do reach 65, our hospitalization is covered by Medicare Part A — a benefit we paid for through our paychecks throughout the years. Yes, there are deductibles and co-payments for long stays in the hospital. And, if you are like most people, you will buy a private Medigap policy or a government-subsidized Medicare advantage plan to pay for those. Or, you may be one of those who are blessed to have retiree health benefits from a previous employer. These programs are very similar to a Medigap policy.

Then, there are outpatient procedures and doctor visits. These are covered by Part B of Medicare. The premium for Part B is normally deducted from your Social Security check. Considering what the benefit pays, the premium is very reasonable.

Again, there is a small deductible and a 20 percent co-pay, covered under most Medigap policies and retirement health plans.

What Is and Isn't Covered

There are other benefits covered under most Medigap policies, including up to 100 days of skilled nursing care. Sometimes people confuse this with long-term care in a skilled nursing facility, and it is a far cry from that. This 100-day coverage is used after a hospital stay of a minimum of three days, and has to be for care classified as "skilled." An example would be speech therapy after a stroke, or rehab after a hip replacement. Once you have plateaued in your recovery, or the 100 days have elapsed, Medicare will no longer pay for your nursing care.

Let's assume you didn't need to go to the hospital for your procedure, or you didn't have surgery requiring skilled care afterward but you still needed care. Maybe you are not physically able to perform some of your normal activities of daily living, such as bathing, dressing, feeding yourself, walking, moving from bed to chair or perhaps you have continence issues. Or it could be that you are having memory issues. Perhaps you have been diagnosed with severe cognitive impairment. In those cases, you will need what is considered custodial care, and Medicare pays no benefits for this. This is where you may need long-term care coverage.

The Big Question

How to pay for long-term care should the need arise is on the minds of many older Americans. What if I buy a policy, pay the premiums for years and never use it? What if I *don't* buy a policy, and then need the coverage? Is the peace of mind knowing my life's savings won't be wiped out by an extended nursing home stay worth paying high premiums for a policy that could cut my benefits and raise my premiums along the way?

The big question is, "Will I need custodial long-term care in my lifetime?" If you knew the answer to that, it would make planning for such an event much easier. You either will or you won't. But you have no crystal ball, and neither do I. What I can tell you is what the statistics say on the matter.

Wade Pfau, professor at The American College and contributor to Forbes magazine, cites research indicating 58 percent of men and 79 percent of women aged 65 and older will need long-term care at some point, and that average lengths for care were 2.2 years for men and 3.7 years for women.[9]

There are several strategies you can implement into your plan to cover these expenses should they occur. One way is to consider buying a long-term care insurance policy.

This has been a popular solution, but it comes at a steep cost. You pay a premium like any other insurance policy. The insurance company is betting that you won't file a claim before you pass away. Through the years they made the underwriting for these policies stricter. This means it's tougher to qualify for the policy if you have pre-existing health conditions. Many companies that in the past have had stellar records of not raising premiums are now, in some cases, announcing substantial rate hikes.

Many insurance companies have dropped out of the long-term care field and no longer offer policies. Why? Because they can't make money. That has left the existing policyholders in a tough situation. When claims rise on the group of policies they have, rates rise along with it. The good news for the consumer is insurance companies must justify rate increases. They must show departments of insurance in the state where they are seeking a rate increase proof that such an increase is warranted. The state could say no. Or they could approve only a portion of the rate increase. The bad news for the consumer is, if the insurance company can't make a profit, they may not offer policies.

If rates go up, the consumer has to decide whether to pay the increase and keep the policy, or let it lapse and lose, not just the coverage, but all the premiums he or she has paid into it.

---

[9] Wade Pfau. Forbes. Jan. 5, 2016. "Costs and Incidence of Long-Term Care." https://www.forbes.com/sites/wadepfau/2016/01/05/costs-and-incidence-of-long-term-care/#6ee329754ceb.

Jerry's Situation

Back in the early 1990s, I met a man named Jerry who was in his 60s. He was a very frugal man and had been a diligent saver all his life. Jerry never lived beyond his means. After his wife died, his children, all of whom lived nearby, would come around often to check on their father to make sure he was doing OK.

A few years ago, Jerry died. Prior to his death, he had been diagnosed with dementia and could not be left alone. The family was faced with a tough decision: how to convince Dad, a man with a strong personality, that he should move into an independent living facility for memory-care patients.

Financially, they had it covered. Jerry had purchased a traditional long-term-care policy that covered the cost of such care. All they needed was proof from a doctor that he needed the care, and a "plan of care" from the facility.

One of Jerry's financial goals was to leave something to his kids and grandkids. The policy's benefits made this possible since it paid for nearly all his care in the facility. His investments remained virtually untouched. When he died, he was able to pass on a substantial inheritance to his three children.

One complaint I hear from listeners on the "Financial Symphony" broadcasts I host, and from attendees at my seminars, is that they tried to file long-term-care claims on their own and found it to be a nightmare. Over the years, I have insisted that my clients please allow us to help them with these claims, whether we provided the policy or not. This lessens the paperwork challenge.

Alternative Choices

Due to the unpredictability of long-term-care claims and other uncertainties associated with traditional long-term-care insurance, consumers have looked at alternative strategies. One alternative strategy is life insurance.

Founding father Benjamin Franklin (1706-1790) once said: "In this world nothing can be said to be certain, except death and taxes." We all know we are going to pass away one day. So, a popular alternative to traditional long-term-care insurance is a permanent life insurance policy that has a chronic illness rider attached. Basically, it works like this. If I have one of these policies, let's say the benefit at death is $500,000 to my beneficiary, then if I become sick and need long-term care — that is to say, I cannot perform at least two activities of daily living mentioned earlier or I experience severe cognitive impairment (memory loss) — then I can file a claim against the $500,000 to pay for my long-term care. Every policy is different, so it is important to thoroughly understand the benefits of the one under consideration. But, typically, if I used the entire amount, I could exhaust my policy. If I don't use the long-term care, the death benefit passes on to the beneficiary or beneficiaries. Unlike conventional long-term-care insurance, where if you don't use it, you lose it (in most cases), with these alternative policies, we all will eventually file a claim on the policy. What is the downside? It is life insurance, and so one of the potential downsides is you have to be fairly healthy to qualify. Most insurance companies have different underwriting criteria. Your financial advisor should be able to ask you a few simple health questions to see if you qualify and which policy would match your individual situation.

For families where insurance doesn't make sense, there are other alternatives. The creation of boosted cash flow to private-pay the health care expense is one. Nowadays, there are income annuities in the marketplace that can facilitate this approach. These products pay a guaranteed lifetime income each month for the rest of your life! While receiving this check, if you become unable to perform the same activities of daily living (ADLs) mentioned earlier, or if you suffer a severe cognitive impairment, the payout in some policies could double the amount of income you receive each month, typically for a limited period of time. This would help with the expense of long-term care whether you were confined to a facility or if you were receiving in-home care.

Not all annuities are created equal, so it is advisable to take your time and thoroughly understand how the benefits and limitations work.

If you served in the military during war time, you may have another option available to you. There is a program called Veteran Affairs (VA) Aid & Attendance that pays the veteran and surviving spouses of veterans a specific amount to help with long-term care in a facility or at home. Of course, there are a lot of qualifications that must be met, but VA specialists can explain whether this benefit applies to you and how to qualify. (It's a good thing that our veterans have some help when it comes to long-term-care needs. They deserve it!)

Lastly, you may want to seek the help of an attorney who specializes in elder care law to design an estate plan to protect as much of your assets allowable by law. This is a specialized area of law. I wouldn't use just any attorney.

The bottom line is this: Health care expenses and long-term-care needs are a crucial piece of the retirement puzzle and can be solved with the right plan in place.

Action Item:

Take the time to learn what method of planning makes sense to your individual situation.

CHAPTER FIVE

How Much Can I Spend?

The greatest good news/bad news story of the 21st century has to do with longevity. The good news is people are living longer these days and, on average, baby boomers will live longer than previous generations.

So, what's the bad news? That people are living longer these days and, on average, baby boomers will live longer than previous generations.

By far the most common concern I hear on our radio show, "The Financial Symphony" is, "How do I know if my money is going to last throughout my retirement?"

It is a legitimate question. When you retire, it's time to enjoy the fruits of your labor, not pinch every nickel until the buffalo squeals. But the thought that runs through the minds of some is that of suddenly becoming a miser as soon as the paychecks stop and they must begin living on their savings.

The average life expectancy is now over 78 years for the first time in American history, and even higher for people who are blessed with good health and good genes, according to data from the Centers for Disease Control.

An article published March 25, 2011, by MarketWatch reported, according to the CDC, a healthy 65-year-old woman has a 50 percent chance of living to age 88, and a 25 percent chance of reaching 94. Statistically, women live longer than men. The CDC estimates a healthy 65-year-old male has a 50 percent chance of seeing 85 and a 25 percent chance of celebrating his 92nd birthday.[10]

Living longer is good, but with extended life expectancy comes some serious retirement planning challenges. Retirements for baby boomers could last 30 years or longer.

DOES THE 4% RULE STILL WORK?

Another difficulty that presents itself to financial advisors is convincing clients they will need three decades of savings.

The MarketWatch article went on to say, "in spite of the statistics and actuarial numbers, only a quarter of retirees and 20 percent of pre-retirees think they'll live to turn 86."

On top of that, there exists a lot of outdated information in the financial world. For years, advisors and financial calculators have been using a withdrawal percentage of 4 percent as a rule of thumb to get you through retirement. They even call it the "4 Percent Withdrawal Rule." Here's the way it works: Say I had

---

[10] Jilian Mincer. MarketWatch. March 25, 2011. "Living Longer: The Good News and Bad." https://www.marketwatch.com/story/living-longer-the-good-news-and-bad-1300983747359.

saved $1 million for retirement and it was invested in a balanced model of stocks and bonds. According to the 4 Percent "Rule," I should feel comfortable withdrawing $40,000 per year and assume with a decent level of probability that my money will last 30 years in retirement. The concept even figures in an amount to compensate for inflation.

Sounds good, right? The only problem is, it doesn't work! The 4 Percent Rule was the brainchild of William Bengen, a California financial advisor, who came up with the formula in the mid-1990s after studying historical stock market returns available to him at the time. That was part of the problem. His data was reflective of a period when the stock market was on a roll. What was not reflected was the tech bubble implosion of 2000 and the financial crisis of 2008. Wall Street loved it. To stockbrokers, it was the Holy Grail of investing.

As the boom years of the 1990s gave way to the "lost decade" of the 2000s, it was back to the drawing board, or at least it should have been. Some financial people refused to recognize that the 4 Percent Rule was dead.

Kelly Greene, a Wall Street Journal financial writer, wrote a fitting obituary for the Bengen formula, "Say Goodbye to the 4% Rule," published March 1, 2013. He put it this way: *"Well, it was beautiful while it lasted. In recent years, the 4 percent rule has been thrown into doubt, thanks to an unexpected hazard: the risk of a prolonged market rout the first two, or even three, years of your retirement. In other words, timing is everything. If your nest egg loses 25 percent of its value just as you start using it, the 4 percent may no longer hold, and the danger of running out of money increases."*[11]

Another problem with the 4 Percent scenario is it assumes cash will pay a fair rate of return like the old days while bonds

---

[11] Kelly Greene. Wall Street Journal. March 3, 2013. "Say Goodbye to the 4% Rule." https://www.wsj.com/articles/say-goodbye-to-the-4-rule-1376315815.

performed well. Well, all of that seems to have changed. As I write this, we have been in an artificially low interest-rate environment. David Blanchett, the head of the financial research organization, Morningstar, contracted Wade Pfau, professor of retirement income at The American College, and Michael Finke, professor of retirement planning and living at Texas Tech University, to produce a research paper on how much retirees should withdraw from their retirement accounts to feel relatively comfortable during a 30-year retirement. Their findings were alarming, to say the least. They recommended 2.8 percent with a balanced portfolio of 40 percent stocks and the rest in bonds and cash. That means the same $1 million retirement portfolio mentioned above that would produce a $40,000 income under the 4 percent formula just got a haircut to $28,000 per year. Ouch! That hurts. Imagine that, a millionaire living on $28,000 per year! But that's the way the numbers crunch if you have your assets invested according to Bengen's formula. [12]

The study went on to say that if you have 80 percent in stocks versus 40 percent, your withdrawal rate should drop to 2.6 percent. Now wait a minute! If stocks have a history of earning more

---

[12] Wade Pfau. Forbes. June 10, 2015. "Safe Withdrawal Rates for Retirement & the Trinity Study." https://www.forbes.com/sites/wadepfau/2015/06/10/safe-with-drawal-rates-for-retirement-and-the-trinity-study/#7de3ecc26fc1.

than bonds and cash, why do you think the study would propose that you spend less? It's simple. When you have 80 percent of your portfolio in equities, you have too much risk and volatility. If you are withdrawing money from a depreciating asset, you are speeding up the depletion of the asset, aren't you? The term for this phenomenon is "reverse-dollar-cost averaging."

Reverse-Dollar-Cost Averaging

Dollar-cost averaging is a friend to the working investor with decades left before retirement. The idea works this way: Every time you receive a paycheck, you contribute a percentage to your 401(k) retirement savings program. The custodians of the plan use that contribution to buy shares of mutual funds in the stock market. When the market is up, the dollars you contribute buy fewer shares that are worth more. When the market is down, your contribution buys more shares that are worth less. But it all averages out (thus the term). As time goes by, the compounding effect of steady investing helps grow the account. So, assuming historical market trends continue, skinny shares eventually fatten up, and your wealth increases on the rising tide.

Everything changes, however, when we sever ourselves from that umbilical paycheck and begin living on our invested funds. Now, instead of *contributing* a set amount each week to our account, we are *withdrawing* from it. Our expenses are constant, so we must withdraw the same amount every week (or month). Every withdrawal means we are selling shares at the prevailing market price. When share prices are down, we are forced to liquidate more shares to create our retirement income. Can you see how a volatile market could work against us? That's reverse-dollar-cost averaging at work.

There are ways to leverage your cash flow and we will spend some time talking about ways to do just that. Professors Finke and Pfau offered some hints in this regard in their research paper. One solution was to possibly consider income annuities because of the leveraging and pooling of money that insurance companies can do. Stay tuned. I will address that later in the book.[13]

A Case in Point

I had a radio caller by the name of Adam come in to visit me. He was a self-investor who called into the program after he heard me talking about the risk of running out of money in retirement. I'm glad he decided to pay me a visit. Upon analyzing his portfolio and his withdrawal percentage, I discovered he was removing 6 percent of his balance annually to cover the expense of maintaining his life-style, and he had 80 percent of his portfolio invested in the stock market.

The good news was the market had been rising, so there was no-harm, no-foul in that regard. But, as we all know, trees don't grow all the way up to Heaven, and the market, regardless of how well things are going today, will eventually experience a correction, or even a crash at some point.

That could have been Adam's fate, but he decided to visit a financial professional just before a market correction. As you might have guessed, he worked out a plan that reduced his risk, created a higher cash flow, and even created extra income for long-term care, if needed. Making the decision to seek help turned out to be a huge benefit in his situation.

---

[13] David Blanchett, Michael Finke and Wade D. Pfau. Morningstar. Jan. 21, 2013. "Low Bond Yields and Safe Portfolio Withdrawal Rates." https://corporate.morningstar.com/US/documents/targetmaturity/LowBondYieldsWithdrawalRates.pdf.

Action Item:

Prepare a budget to see how much you will need to spend monthly from your invested savings. This will enable us to see if your retirement will last 30 years. If it seems overwhelming, or the numbers do not add up, our financial roadmap will tell you specifically what your withdrawal percentages should be.

CHAPTER SIX

Why a Fiduciary?

N ow, there is a word you don't use in everyday conversation — fiduciary. Pronounced *fuh-DOO-she-urry.* What does it mean?

Fiduciary comes from a Latin word, *fidere,* meaning "to trust." Some similar words with the same root we use more often are fidelity, confidentiality and confidence.

According to Investopedia, the legal definition of fiduciary is "a person or organization that owes to another the duties of good faith and trust. The highest legal duty of one party to another, it also involves being bound ethically to act in the other's best interests."

You would think this would be automatic, wouldn't you? But as I write this, the U.S. Department of Labor has once again delayed enforcing a new rule that *requires* anyone who dispenses financial advice to be a fiduciary.

America prides itself on being a bastion of free enterprise. And it is! But along with that comes some potential land mines that call to mind another Latin expression: Caveat Emptor, "Let the buyer beware." Nearly anyone these days can set up shop and hang out a shingle declaring himself or herself to be a "financial advisor."

According to Tony Robbins, famous American author, entrepreneur, philanthropist and life coach, there are an estimated 310,000 financial professionals in the United States and most of them are *not* fiduciaries. In a 2017 interview with Money magazine, Robbins said that 90 percent of financial professionals are brokers.

The way things have stood for years, stockbrokers owe their first loyalty to the brokerage houses they represent, not their clients. Brokers are held to the less strict and vaguer "suitability" standard. The suitability standard calls for the financial professional to merely believe the investment he or she is recommending will not *harm* the client — not that it is necessarily the one in the client's best interest.

A "broker" is by definition one who puts a buyer together with a seller to make a sale. Take real estate brokers, for example. Ask a real estate broker which house out of all those on the market is the best one for you. It would be naïve to think the real estate agent would suggest a property that would rob them of their commission. You don't go to a Toyota dealership to buy a Ford.

Some financial professionals may have a desire to be helpful, but are unable to provide guidance with expertise and training they don't possess. As philosopher Abraham Maslow said, "If the only tool you have is a hammer, you tend to see every problem as a nail." Stockbrokers are trained in equities, just as insurance agents are trained in insurance. Yet, both sometimes bill themselves as financial advisors. Chiropractors and surgeons are both in the medical field, but each is likely to recommend a regime of treatment from their training and field of expertise. You can't expect stockbrokers to recommend alternative investment strategies that contain no market risk to their clients — *even those close to or in retirement.* It is just not in their wheelhouse.

To continue with the medical metaphor, a competent holistic physician will look at the person as a whole and not just treat an isolated symptom. Before prescribing medicine, a holistic physician may ask hundreds of questions to get the entire picture before recommending any form of treatment.

Or, to tie this back into the concept of a symphony, in practice, a musical conductor will not only listen to the tubas. Nor will he only take time to work with violins. Rather, he will dedicate himself to listening, working with and fine-tuning each section, each musician, in the hopes of securing a fully balanced orchestra.

A fiduciary financial advisor does the same thing with your financial well-being. In fact, with a fiduciary, it is a legal obligation to do so.

I find the biggest mistake folks make when they move into retirement is not getting a full analysis of their current financial situation. The financial landscape of retirement can be a confusing place. They don't feel capable of navigating it themselves, so they seek professional help — someone in the financial services business. They assume the individual has their best interests at heart. But if they are dealing with a salesperson for stocks, bonds and mutual funds, they could learn the hard way the dangers of making assumptions. Oh, sure, the "salesperson" may ask a handful of questions having to do with risk, and talk about balance and diversification, but at the end of the day, if all the assets are in equities and none of the assets are in alternative investments, your portfolio may be characterized by too much risk and with more many charges and fees than you should have for your financial timeline.

Most Are Unaware of Fees

Robbins makes the point that 71 percent of Americans think they pay nothing for their 401(k), and nothing could be further from the truth. He adds that 92 percent of those who know they have fees associated with their retirement accounts don't know how much they are. Robbins says the average fee for a 401(k) is 3.2 percent, and every percentage point above 1 percent represents about 10 years income.[14,15]

Fiduciaries are your advocate. They won't be answering to a broker dealer as to what investments to recommend. Fiduciaries are required by law to be transparent about fees.

Enactment of the new DOL regulations has sparked debate. There are those in Congress and other prominent politicians who are against implementation of the new ruling. When we started managing investments for families there were no such rules being discussed. To us, it was a no-brainer. We made the conscious decision to be fiduciaries because we feel strongly that a fiduciary relationship naturally reflects our morals and ethics.

[14] Lona Choi-Allum. AARP. March 2011. "401(k) Participants' Awareness and Understanding of Fees." https://www.aarp.org/work/retirement-planning/info-02-2011/401k-fees-awareness-11.html.

[15] Susan Lyon. NerdWallet. April 2, 2013. "Study: 9 in 10 Americans Underestimate Their Hidden 401(k) Fees." https://admin.emeraldconnect.com/files/71336/401k%20Study.pdf.

Ronald Reagan, president of the U.S. back in the 1980s, was negotiating with the Soviets on arms control. He was a master of making a point with few words. He knew that it was part of Russian culture to speak with many proverbs. In negotiating with Mikhail Gorbachev, then leader of the U.S.S.R., over the wording of a treaty to limit the production and deployment of nuclear missiles, President Reagan used a phrase that was a favorite of the founder of communism, Vladimir Lenin: *"Doveryai, no proveryai,"* the English translation of which is, *"Trust but verify."* The expression was picked up by the press and became a signature phrase of the negotiations.

The wisdom of such a proverb is obvious. Whenever money is involved, it is prudent to do your due diligence before signing the dotted line. Ask as many questions as you can think of, and then ask others with experience and expertise what questions you should have asked.

Investing your life's savings is serious business. Emotions are involved. Trust should be earned. To borrow an expression from poker players, "Trust everybody, but cut the cards." When it comes to choosing the right advisor or financial coach, don't be afraid to ask questions until you are satisfied they are working with your best interests at heart. One of the first and most important questions to ask is, "Are you a fiduciary?"

If the response is, "Am I a what?" it may be an indication that you are in the wrong place.

If the answer you get is long and rambling, or you start hearing reasons why it's not important to deal with a fiduciary, again, you may be talking to the wrong person.

What you want to hear is a direct and simple "yes" answer, followed by an interview during which the financial advisor asks many questions. Why? Because, as we stated earlier, the job of a fiduciary is to work in your best interests, without regard to his personal interests. How could he or she know what your best interests are without such an open and forthright discussion?

Commissions and Remuneration

This is not to say fiduciaries do not earn a living at what they do. If they are successful at what they do, they should be able to help many people and thus earn a healthy income. This is America, after all, where we expect to pay professionals what they are worth if they render valuable services to us.

Think of a travel agency, for example. They can usually save you lots of money if you are taking a two-week vacation in the Caribbean. Why? Because they can shop for the best price on hotels and airlines. They are not beholding to any of the vendors they use to put your travel package together. But it would be naïve to think they are not compensated. In fact, they are paid by the airlines and hotels they use. But in the end, they work for you. You don't mind, because you are the one who benefits in the long run. Commission is not a dirty word. Money managers who have a stake in the growth of your portfolio are motivated to produce success for you.

From an early age, you were probably taught that it is rude to ask someone outright, "How much money do you make?" But asking your financial advisor *how* he or she gets paid is not rude.

To quote a line from the 1973 movie, "The Godfather," "It's not personal; it's business." It is also a good way to find out whether you are working with a fiduciary who will put your interests first. In the investing world, for instance, it is a violation of both the suitability standard and the fiduciary standard if stockbrokers misuse their relationship with a client by "churning." That's the term used for trading in excess within a portfolio just to earn extra commissions. How do you know if you have been a victim of churning? Look at your account statement. Brokerage firms are required to send you confirmations of every transaction. If you notice an excess of trading activity, ask about it.

Sometimes new, prospective clients come in for a consultation and, at some point in the conversation, tell me they have been with an advisor for years and they like and trust him or her.

"Is your advisor a fiduciary?" I will ask. They don't know.

"How does your advisor get paid?" I will ask. They don't know.

You should know. Not because you are nosy, but because you want to ferret out any conflict of interests that may influence their recommendations. Consider this: If your advisor is remunerated only when he or she sells you something or makes changes within your portfolio, could that possibly influence their recommendations? Would knowing the answer to those questions affect the level of confidence you have in your advisor's recommendations? If they say they are paid by fee only, is it OK to ask how much the fee is and how it is structured, who pays it, and how often they receive it? You bet it is!

To revisit the travel agent analogy, on the occasions when I have used them to book my travel arrangements, I have sat at their desk and watched the agents clicking away at their computers squeezing out every dollar to make sure I got the best fare and lodging rate available. They also seemed very interested in my preferences and needs. I knew they got paid by vendors, but I did not get the impression that was driving their decisions. It was obvious they were working for me.

If the advisor candidate you are interviewing for the job of looking after your life's savings seems unwilling to answer questions about compensation quickly and clearly, run!

Action Item:

Ask questions to make sure you are hiring the right advisor/coach.

CHAPTER SEVEN

Diversify, Diversify, Diversify

'm sure you have heard the axiom, "Don't put all your eggs in one basket." It means don't risk everything you have on the success of one venture. Don't concentrate all of your assets in one place or one thing, or you could lose everything. Spread it around so if one thing goes south you have the other "baskets" to preserve the whole.

This adage is especially true in investing. Concentrating all your resources in one segment of the market could cost you everything. Spreading it out over noncorrelated securities that serve to counterbalance one another can help protect the nest egg by keeping the value even. Big businesses diversify — at least, the smart ones do.

For example, let's say Giant Holdings, Inc. owns several retail outlets. One is a high-end department store we will call Major Bucks. When the economy is booming, Major Bucks does very well. But because Giant Holdings, Inc. knows the economy does not always perform at an optimum, it creates a chain of discount stores they call Sensible-N-Cheap. These stores cater to customers who want to pay as little as possible for items they need. If the economy moves into a recession, Major Bucks sales will decline. They know that. They also know that Sensible-N-Cheap's sales will boom and pick up the slack.

If you are an investor and you want to diversify, you will put your money into segments of the market that can produce profits in a similar fashion. When one is down, market forces will cause the other to rise.

I was asked by the Wall Street Journal how we implement this type of strategy, so I know I am not the only advisor/coach who uses this style of planning.

Path to Diversification

A client we will call Dave told me of his experience after he had received a sizable sum of cash as an inheritance from a relative. He knew he had to put the money to work somewhere, but he had little knowledge of investing. The amount was just north of $300,000. He looked in the yellow pages under investments and, with his cashier's check in a locked briefcase, he headed for the offices of the first company he came across. When he entered the double doors of the glass tower, he was impressed by the marble tile in the foyer, the modern furniture and the friendly receptionist, who chirped cheerily, "Just have a seat and one of our investment advisors will be right with you."

In a few minutes, a young woman rounded the corner, greeted him, and directed him to a well-appointed conference room with a large, flat-screen display connected to a computer terminal.

Dave's question was simple: "How should I invest my money?" In answer, the investment counselor showed Dave three pie charts, each representing what she said was differing degrees of risk.

Chart One (the riskiest) had Dave's investment divided as follows:
- 50% growth stocks (high growth potential but high risk)

- 15% large cap stocks
- 15% small cap stocks
- 10% international stocks
- 10% money market

Chart Two was divided as follows:
- 30% growth stocks
- 20% small cap stocks
- 20% large cap stocks
- 10% money market
- 10% certificates of deposit.

Chart Three was the most conservative:
- 10% growth stocks
- 35% small cap stocks
- 35% large cap stocks
- 10% money market
- 10% certificates of deposit

"Either way, you are diversified," the woman told Dave. Dave had heard diversification was a smart thing to do when investing, so he opened the account with the large investment firm, and chose the middle pie chart.

Then 2008 happened. Dave lost 37 percent of his investment in a matter of weeks. Was Dave diversified? Not really. Nearly all his investments were in equities, subject to the ebb and flow of the stock market.

"Don't worry," his investment advisor told him. "When the tide goes out, all the boats go down. When it comes back, all boats rise."

That sounded good. But anyone who lived through the financial crisis of 2008 can tell you it was no normal ebb and flow of market activity. The tide didn't just recede for the day and then return. It was as if the entire ocean left the pier! As this book is written, it has been nearly a decade since 2008, and I know of some who have not fully recovered from that devastating event.

In Dave's case, he was 60 years old when he deposited his money in the glass tower investment firm. The financial crisis hit two years later. That close to retirement, Dave did not have time to wait for the market to bounce back. He was counting on that money to augment his Social Security, his 401(k) and his meager savings to help him retire.

True diversification is not just spreading your assets across a variety of different stocks or using multiple brokerages, it is investing in a variety of asset classes — reducing risk by dispersing the investment among dissimilar assets. For example, it is a fact, when the economy is on a roll, people travel more. Let's say an investor bought shares of stock in several hotel chains. Would that classify as true diversification? No. That investor is "all in," you might say, in the hospitality industry. When a market correction comes along, profits in that industry can stall across the board, and that investor can lose money. Sectors that fare well in recessionary times could be health care, consumer staples and utilities. These are things people will buy regardless of whether times are good or bad. Investing in both the hotel industry and, say, the health care industry would make the investor more diversified.

Start With a "Rainy Day" Fund

True diversification starts with an emergency basket, or a "rainy day" fund. This could be cash at a bank or credit union. No, it's not going to pay much interest, not right now as I write this, anyway. But that is not the top priority with an emergency fund. Ready access is. In an emergency, you need to be able to get to your money quickly.

What is this "rainy day" fund for? You name it! A tree falls on your roof and you have a high deductible on your homeowner's insurance policy. The old family car finally gave up the ghost and you have to replace it tomorrow. A sudden illness. A death in the family requiring expensive air fare. The last thing you want to do is withdraw money from your savings. You also don't want to borrow the money or use credit.

How much should you place in your emergency fund? Well, that is up to you, but I recommend parking at least three to six months of living expenses in this basket. Why? If you are still working and you lose your job, you may need at least that amount to tide you over until you can find other work. You don't want to inflate your emergency fund by too much because of the low or perhaps nonexistent interest paid on such liquid accounts. If you can access hundreds of dollars from an ATM machine, chances are these funds are not tied to a hefty interest rate. Even savings accounts containing hundreds of thousands of dollars these days don't beat inflation. So, you are losing spending power. That's the reason for limiting the amount in this basket. But it is just the responsible thing to do to start here.

Formula for Diversification

In a perfect scenario, retirement could last 30 years or more. For this reason, I would suggest having a comfortable percentage in a disciplined, diversified portfolio designed to grow ahead of the prevailing inflation rate, but also with enough fixed income sprinkled in the model to manage risk. This is what I call "diversified growth."

Here's a typical example of a model we use for our clients that has worked well for them in the long term: For a retiree, we may keep 50 percent in equities (stocks) and 50 percent in fixed income. When I say stocks, I'm not talking about shares in the 30 blue-chip companies that make up the Dow (Dow Jones Industrial Average), or stock in the 500 large-cap companies that make up the S&P (Standard & Poors) 500. I'm talking about a truly diversified portfolio that has *thousands* of stocks invested globally with *many different sectors* and *sizes* of companies. This is to grow money as a hedge against inflation.

Instead of picking sectors (and picking incorrectly), this academic approach (and one which has won a Nobel prize) is designed to stay invested in all sectors and let the market grow it for the long term. To maximize that growth, an aggressive rebalancing strategy is maintained to enhance performance. It is the best use of the old buy-low-sell-high investing philosophy that has done so well for billionaire market mavens like Berkshire Hathaway CEO Warren Buffet.

I use the word discipline in describing this portfolio. Why? Because when the stock market is dropping because of normal volatility, or perhaps because the economy is weakening, staying invested is not for the faint of heart. But by buying while it's dropping, you are adding shares to the portfolio. Not only does it grow back faster, it eliminates one of the most common investor mistakes — bad market timing. When do I get out? When do I get back in? I hear horror stories of money managers who try to time the market and get this one wrong, let alone the self-investor who, ruled by emotion, finds it a hair-raising challenge and usually guesses wrong. The disciplined approach uses computer-assisted math and calculative formulas, not gut instincts, to make such moves.

Asset Allocation

A client came into my office last year. He said, "Mark. I've been invested in cash since the 2008 stock market crash. I know I've missed out on recent gains. I need a plan."

I felt so sorry for him. Yep, he missed out on the second-longest bull market that posted gains of over 300 percent. The proposed solution for him was using a diversified investing strategy such as the one described before. This could help him manage his future risk so that his urge to jump out of the market could be diminished.

"For the long-term investor, asset allocation is the primary determinant of returns," says Roger G. Ibbotson, an emeritus professor at Yale School of Finance who founded Ibbotson Associates. Ibbotson has made a life's work out of studying the science of marketing investing. He is often asked to speak at universities, forums and conferences, and has enough financial degrees from prestigious universities to paper an office wall.

In a nutshell, asset allocation involves using three asset classes — stocks, bonds and cash (and cash equivalents) — so the investor can take advantage of their diversity. These three components have differing levels of risk and return. They will each behave differently in different market environments. Stocks will generally average the highest returns over time, but they will also be more volatile, and hence have more risk — perhaps double that of bonds. Cash, the big safety valve, fluctuates little and returns little, but serves as a counter-balance to equities.[16]

Most Fund Managers Are Unsuccessful

Like sports heroes when they are on top of their games, when mutual fund managers have a great year, they are touted as gurus and prescient seers who can predict the stock market. Such is far from the truth.

SPIVA is an acronym for "S&P Indices Versus Active." It is a research scorecard issued by an investing think tank every six

---

[16] Rachael Tay. Grow Your Capital. January 2008. "Asset Allocation in a Nutshell." http://www.gyc.com.sg/files/0801_asset.pdf.

months that keeps an eye on the performance of actively managed mutual funds investing in stock market equities, as well as fixed income. SPIVA compares the investing success of fund managers against their respective benchmarks, such as the S&P Index and the DJIA Index. Since 2002, this scorecard has been one of the best litmus tests to determine how well mutual fund managers are performing. If they don't beat the index, are they really worth the fees they charge to manage your money? If you answered no, go to the head of the class.

In 2015, for example, when the S&P Index posted a paltry total return of 1.4 percent (with dividends included) 66 percent of "actively managed" large-company stock funds posted smaller returns than the index. What?!! You mean two out of three fund managers underperformed the stock benchmark against which they are measured? Yep.

According to a USA Today article by Adam Shell in March 2016, "the longer-term outlook is just as gloomy, with 84 percent of large-cap funds generating lower returns than the S&P 500 in the latest five-year period and 82 percent falling shy in the past 10 years.[17]

So, if you are relying on having the right mutual fund to grow your retirement without being diversified, you may be seriously disappointed. Therefore, we prefer the disciplined, *truly* diversified investment strategies.

When mutual fund managers are being hailed as seers and investment prognosticators, the inference is past performance is a reliable indicator of future results. Nothing could be further from the truth. In fact, we were surprised to learn just how many funds start with a sizzle and then end with a fizzle, never to be heard from again.

---

[17] Adam Shell. USA Today. March 14, 2016. "66% of fund managers can't match S&P results." https://www.usatoday.com/story/money/personal-finance/2016/03/14/66-fund-managers-cant-match-sp-results/81644182/.

One study revealed mutual fund data indicates many funds don't last as long as their investors. Daniel S. Kern, Chief Investment Officer of TFC Financial Management, observes, "Of the funds in operation in 1995, less than 40 percent still existed in 2013. The remaining funds were either closed or merged into other funds."

Kern feels, while industry insiders downplay the implications of these closures and mergers, it is not good news for investors.

"At best, closure or merger of a fund is an inconvenience that forces the investor to make a new investment decision," Kern says. "At worst, the fund closure or merger may lead to adverse consequences. Fund closures and mergers can create tax consequences or transaction costs that the investor doesn't control."

Here's something many mutual fund investors don't realize. When a dying fund merges with a surviving fund, there are often additional costs connected with the merger or closure absorbed by the new fund. These costs can reduce returns due the investor.[18]

As fiduciaries, we are always evaluating different investing strategies that can benefit our clients. If there is a more efficient way, we want to add that strategy to our investing arsenal. We are also firm believers that there are other buckets of money that diversify your retirement nest egg. For example, income-producing buckets are needed when you retire — a concept we will talk about in some detail in the next couple of chapters.

---

[18] Daniel S. Kern. ThinkAdvisor. Nov. 14, 2013. "Will Your Mutual Fund Die Before You Do?" http://www.thinkadvisor.com/2013/11/14/will-your-mutual-fund-die-before-you-do.

Action Item:

Have an overlap report produced on your portfolio to see just how diversified it is, and a "stress test" to see if you are currently achieving a high enough reward for the risk you are taking.

CHAPTER EIGHT

Another Name for Retirement: Permanent Unemployment!

My mother and father are both amazing people.

As I write this, Dad is 92 and Mom is 89 and they still live by themselves in Dothan, Alabama. Why there? Well, my sister lives in Florida, and my brother lives in Birmingham, Alabama. I live in Atlanta, Georgia. My parents decided more than 20 years ago they wanted to live in Dothan because it was an equal distance from each of us.

One major reason they have been able to maintain their independence is their good health up until now. But that's not the whole story. Another contributing factor to their continued independence is they both retired with pension checks that provide cost-of-living increases to supplement their Social Security checks. Mom and Dad could essentially replace their paychecks when they retired.

My father worked many years for the State of Delaware, and my mother has a pension from the DuPont Corporation. My father's pension check ended up being more than his salary. There came a time when it actually cost him money to go to work! That's how good his pension program was! You just can't find situations like that anymore.

HAPPY RETIREMENT

But that is the goal, isn't it? To replace our paycheck when we retire and continue to maintain the lifestyle in post-retirement that we did in the days before we retired? Big companies and other employment organizations these days are unwilling to provide lucrative pensions like the ones my father and mother receive. Pensions are going the way of the Dodo Bird and the hula-hoop. So, what happened to them?

The Disappearance of Pensions

Does anybody remember the Studebaker? It was a sleek and powerful automobile that, in the 1950s, was slightly ahead of its time in terms of performance and safety. The Studebaker was, in fact, the first production automobile to have seat belts and padded dashboards.

Henry and Clem Studebaker were blacksmiths in the mid-1800s, but their brother, John, caught gold fever and struck out for California to claim his fortune. Once he got to California, he discovered he could earn more money by making wheelbarrows and wagons than he could mining for gold. In 1852, he returned to South Bend, Indiana, with $8,000 and joined his brothers in the Studebaker Wagon Corporation. In 1901, after his brothers had died, John Studebaker visited a motor show in Chicago and decided to build an all-electric horseless carriage. The gas-powered models came along in 1904. By 1909, Studebaker had made almost $10 million (over $270 million today) selling cars with internal combustion engines.

What does all this have to do with pensions, Mark?

Bear with me, OK? Even though it was fast and well-built and futuristic in design, the Studebaker reached a point where it just didn't sell. By the time the 1960s rolled around, the Studebaker Corporation was closing factories and laying off its employees, wholesale. The last Studebaker was manufactured in the spring of 1966.

Studebaker had a great pension program. Too good, in fact. They quickly discovered they couldn't pay their discharged workers what they had promised. Auto workers howled and took it to the news media and Congress. In the 1970s, a general recession caused other car manufacturers to close plants and send workers home. This pushed matters to a head. Congress passed the Employee Retirement Income Security Act of 1974 (ERISA). The law's goal was to regulate pension plans and hold employers' feet to the fire and make them fulfill their pension promises. But it ended up causing companies to scrap pensions altogether.

All of this served to dramatically change the way Americans looked at their financial security in retirement. Instead of working for a company for four decades and getting a pension and a gold watch, workers came to realize they would have to provide their own pension through individual savings.

ERISA created something new — IRAs and 401(k)s. These do-it-yourself retirement savings plans were designed to incentivize companies with tax credits and entice workers with tax deferment. Every dollar you contributed to your plan (up to a limit set by the IRS) was a dollar the IRS wouldn't tax you on until you withdrew it. These new programs were called "defined-*contribution* plans," as opposed to the "defined-*benefit* plans," as pensions were called.

Pension plans were supposed to be guaranteed by the company, corporation or entity offering them. Like my father and mother, people could retire with peace of mind, knowing their pension check would always be in the mailbox on the proscribed day. There were no such guarantees with 401(k)-type plans. These depended on the success of the investments the workers selected and the regularity with which they contributed to their plans.

The good news was these defined-contribution plans were tax-deferred. The gains in the plan would grow untaxed, thus producing more accelerated growth than an ordinary investment. The bad news was (a) you, not your employer, were responsible for creating and managing your nest egg, and (b) during a market reversal, you could lose money. For someone on the cusp of retirement, a market crash could be devastating.

Lest we confuse tax-deferred with tax-free, Uncle Sam is no fool. The government will get his cut — likely a much bigger one — when withdrawal time comes. Just to make sure you withdraw your money from these tax-deferred retirement programs (often called "qualified" plans), the IRS has put into place something called RMDs (required minimum distributions). These rules force you to withdraw an ever-increasing percentage from these accounts when you reach 70 ½ years old.

IRAs have become very popular. Millions of Americans have pumped trillions of dollars into them. IRA owners were delighted to see their taxes shrink and their retirement savings compound quicker during the accumulation phase of their lives. But when they enter the distribution phase (retirement) they discover the IRA has a little more complexity than they first imagined. Passing their assets to their heirs can be tricky. If they don't do it intelligently, the IRS can claim almost half of it for the tax coffers.

Publication 590, or "Pub 590" for short, is the section of the Internal Revenue Service code that deals with IRAs. Publication 590 is not for beach reading. It is 110 pages long and contains the rules for IRAs. Leading IRA expert Ed Slott writes in his book, "The Retirement Savings Time Bomb ... and How to Defuse It":

> "Due to a complex combination of distribution and estate taxes that kick in at retirement or death, millions of you are at risk of losing much — perhaps even most — of your retirement savings."

Variations Emerge

Ever heard of U.S. Senator William V. Roth? He represented Delaware, the state of my childhood, in the U.S. Senate. He became famous as a fiscal conservative who sponsored legislation to create retirement savings accounts that would be taxed up front, but not on the back end. Forward-thinking savers now pump money into Roth IRAs, Roth 401(k)s, Roth 403(b)s and the like. Senator Roth maintained that the less we have to pay in taxes, the more we will spend and save, which would, in turn, stimulate the economy. This, he claimed, would generate more revenue for the government in the long run than a direct tax would. The Taxpayer Relief Act of 1997, which was his idea, allows you to pay the taxes on the front end of Roth IRA and Roth 401(k), allow it to grow and be distributed tax-free. Today, Roth IRAs can be set up at many financial institutions and insurance companies, and more and more employers are offering Roth 401(k)s. They allow for early withdrawal of your original contribution (not the earnings) without penalties after a five-year waiting period. The earnings generated from the original Roth IRA contribution can also be withdrawn early, but the earnings are subject to penalties.

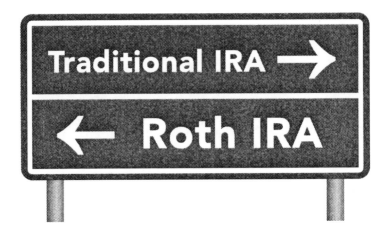

Keep in mind, all of this is a broad-brush explanation of these programs. Rules are constantly changing, so see me in person for details. But the takeaway from all of this is we are the ones who must provide our own "pensions" these days. Neither the government nor our employer will do it for us.

A Balancing Act

If the market grows and we are diversified, our market investments should grow, too. If the market is flat, or spiralling downward, our market investments may drop with it. How do we balance that out? Through income-producing holdings, higher interest and dividends, so that if the market is flat, the dividends and interest combine to grow the portfolio and, if we are retired, create income.

I covered reverse-dollar-cost averaging in Chapter Five of this book. Many retirees find themselves in a position of having to sell when the market is down to create a paycheck. You never want to sell if the market is down. That's called locking in your losses. You can't recover locked losses. That's why an income-

and-growth blend of holdings can be used as a diversifier when the markets are stagnant. In such periods, reinvested interest and dividends add to the portfolio.

It is crucial to continue to diversify this model as well. We don't want our income to be just dividends from stocks, because that could put us right back on the big roller coaster we don't want to ride in retirement. It simply makes sense to have a diversified model capable of generating interest and dividends from a diverse group of holdings, dividends, fixed income and alternative investments. When you add potential growth to that model, you benefit twice — income and growth.

The downside to any model that has market exposure is you will see volatility. This is where I've seen advisors make major mistakes. Why? Because they simply don't ask enough questions to gauge their client's comfort level. If the portfolio is adjusted to the client's comfort level, when volatility increases, the investor's nervousness shouldn't increase. The client knows what to expect. He or she is comfortable with some volatility and will not be tempted to cash out while the market is down. Instead of selling low and buying high, they will be prudent investors, understanding how their assets are allocated, and at peace with the process.

Action Item:

Have your risk tolerance analyzed. Complete a financial roadmap to evaluate how much risk is needed (mathematically speaking) to help you achieve your financial goals.

CHAPTER NINE

"I Hate Annuities"?

The production team for our radio and television show, "The Financial Symphony," gets all kind of questions from our listeners all over the country. They love it when someone calls in and says, "My broker is recommending that I move my 401(k) into a variable annuity. *What do you think I should do?*"

Fire your financial advisor. That's what I think you should do.

I'm not a fan of variable annuities. There is a reason. I have run fee reports on some of these policies. It is not unusual for the investor/policyholder to be paying anywhere from 3–5 percent annually in fees! Are you kidding me? Every dollar you pay in fees eats away at the returns, so it is no wonder these investments often yield so poorly.

If the broker wants to sell you a variable annuity, he or she will tell you all the benefits you obtain by paying those fees. I get that. But I also know there are other kinds of annuities that provide similar benefits for a *fraction* of the cost! The annuities I have in mind might have less upside potential, but they also don't have the downsides of the market.

I don't know about you, but when it comes to spending money, value received for money spent is a big consideration. I don't consider myself to be cheap, but I hate wasting money. I realize there are always fees involved when you are talking about financial products. After all, we live in a free enterprise system, and professionals need to charge for their services. I think most of our clients here at Lloyd Advisory Services understand no one works for free. But there is a big difference in reasonable fees for services rendered and overcharging.

Let me be clear. I am not an annuity hater. As a matter of fact, I own some annuities in my own retirement accounts — just not variable annuities. You can sum up the answer to why annuities exist, and why they may have a place in your retirement portfolio, in one word — income. Unlike my parents, who had pensions, I fall into the category of individuals without a guaranteed income stream at retirement. So, I had to create my own "pension."

In Chapter Five of this book, I referred to a Morningstar white paper published by Wade Pfau and Michael Finke in 2013 that discussed safe portfolio withdrawal rates from a market-based investment account. These researchers concluded the numbers simply don't add up for proponents of the 4 percent withdrawal theory. Pulling 4 percent from your portfolio may allow you to live well for a few years, but you have a 50 percent chance of running out of money.

After crunching the numbers, Pfau and Finke say retirees who want their retirements to last 30 years must increase their savings by 42.9 percent and lower their initial withdrawal rate to 2.8 percent. For most folks, that's some severe belt-tightening.[19]

This makes the contractual cash flow guarantees built into income annuities attractive. Some of these contracts offer 4–5 percent withdrawal rates — and in some cases higher — to create a guaranteed income stream.

---

[19] David Blanchett, Michael Finke and Wade D. Pfau. Morningstar. Jan. 21, 2013. "Low Bond Yields and Safe Portfolio Withdrawal Rates." https://corporate.morningstar.com/US/documents/targetmaturity/LowBondYieldsWithdrawalRates.pdf.

When considering purchasing an annuity, always look at the financials of the insurance company offering the contract. The best way to determine the financial strength of an insurance company is to consult independent insurance rating services such as A.M. Best, Standard and Poor's, Fitch and Moody's. Just like consumer credit rating organizations will have a slightly different score for the same individual, insurance company rating organizations may sometimes vary. But, in general, they are consistently close. These organizations evaluate the past performance of a carrier based on their analysis of historical data, and examine other key factors, such as strength of financial reserves, management style and claims-payment history. Then they come up with report-card-style grades.

When an insurance company is "A-rated," it means that carrier is financially sound and creditworthy. In other words, it has the financial strength necessary to pay claims and repay creditors. These independent rating organizations give ratings of "C" or "D" to companies they consider to be financially weak compared to their peers in the industry.

Not All Annuities are Alike

All sedans are automobiles, but not all automobiles are sedans. There is so much difference between variable annuities and fixed annuities that one of them should be renamed to avoid confusion.

In my discussions with people about how to establish a guaranteed income in retirement, I sometimes ask them what they think of annuities. More often than not, I get a negative response. But if I describe what an income annuity does without mentioning it by name, the response is most often positive. What does that say about our perceptions of annuities? That we sometimes build our opinions before we know the facts? I would agree with that.

Scenario: Uncle Robert, who had a bad experience with a *variable* annuity, mentions to nephew John that he loathes annuities, and advises him to avoid them like the plague. John shares the opinion with his brother, Mike. Neither of them bother to read up on annuities and learn they are not all the same. All they know is, they have it from a reliable source (Uncle Robert) that annuities are not to be trusted.

Let's start with a little history. The word "annuity" is derived from the Latin "annus," meaning year. Soldiers of ancient Rome were paid well. Of course, it was dangerous work, fighting Gauls and Huns, so they pooled their money so, if one of them fell, the fund would take care of their families back home. The stipend was paid yearly, thus the name. The idea caught on with the general public and it soon became a business. In his book, "Pay Checks and Play Checks," author Tom Hegna says in A.D. 225, a Roman judge produced the first known mortality table, enabling lifetime yearly stipends to be made for a lump sum. Fast forward a few centuries to the 1700s, and we see the British Parliament authorizing the sale of annuities to people of "high society as prevention from humiliation should their families 'fall from grace.'"

America adopted the idea in 1776 with the adoption by Congress of the National Pension Program, which provided annuity payments to soldiers and their families. In 1905, Andrew Carnegie established the Teacher's Pension Fund, which eventually became the Teacher's Insurance and Annuity Association (TIAA) in 1918 to provide annuities to teachers.[20]

Variable annuities are stock market investments in an insurance wrapper. The idea originated in the 1950s to accommodate

---

[20] Marvin Feldman and Maria Wood. May 8, 2012. "Slideshow: The History of Annuities." http://www.thinkadvisor.com/2012/05/08/slideshow-the-history-of-annuities.

tax deferral and incorporate contractual benefits that only insurance companies could provide — at a cost, of course.

Variable annuities have separate accounts that invest in different sectors of the economy. When you pick these accounts, you are exposing yourself to different levels of risk. Your contract value will go up and down with the market if you are invested in equities. So, what differentiates a variable annuity from a plain old stock market investment? Inside the variable annuity, you can use after-tax money and it grows tax-deferred. You usually have a surrender period that ties the balance up for a time, except for penalty-free withdrawals. That, in addition to the fees, is one of the biggest complaints I hear from folks who have bought variable annuities.

Riders are available (at more costs) to guarantee interest for the use of creating a lifetime income. Death benefit riders are available, but they are taxable. With variable annuities, the fees keep adding up.

Fixed annuities are somewhat like a certificate of deposit — but with an insurance company instead of a bank, and typically at higher rates of return than a bank offers. Money invested in a CD are insured by the Federal Deposit Insurance Corporation (FDIC). Fixed annuities are not insured by the FDIC but are linked to the insurer's general account, and are as sound as the financial health of the insurance company.

Traditional fixed annuities do not use a market index to calculate your interest. Those are fixed index annuities. We will get to those later. Traditional fixed annuities offer a contractually guaranteed interest rate. That means you know how much your account will earn each year. Historically, the rates of return have been higher than bank CDs, but how much higher depends on the company.

Another difference between CDs and fixed annuities is tax deferral. If you fund a fixed annuity with after-tax money, the interest will not generate a 1099, as the asset grows tax-deferred.

Why is this a good thing? Because not only does your principal earn interest but, in most cases, your interest earns interest as well. You will pay income tax on the interest when you start withdrawing the interest, however — most likely at retirement.

It is not wise to use money you will soon need to purchase an annuity. These are long-term financial products. Think of a financial time capsule. You put the money in and let it earn interest until you need to withdraw it in the form of income, or possibly a lump sum. And, of course, always check the financials of the insurance company before buying an annuity.

Immediate annuities are similar to an income annuity. You give a lump-sum premium payment to an insurance company, and they give you a regular monthly check for a period of time. Depending on the contract, it can be for a specific period — say 10 years or 20 years — or for the rest of your life. A word of caution: If you choose a lifetime payout, and then die six months later, the insurance company can keep the money. For this reason, I am not a big fan of immediate annuities. There are other types of annuities that offer lifetime income and, when you die, whatever is left in the contract goes to your beneficiary. Those types of annuities give you the income you need but protect your beneficiaries as well.

Fixed index annuities were created in the mid-1990s as a new breed of fixed annuity. The fixed index annuity was designed, first and foremost, to help you create a guaranteed stream of income for as long as you live, but also affords you the additional benefits of protection from market losses and limited access to the annuity contract's value if needed. I call this a "protected income annuity" because:

1. Your principal is protected from losses in the stock market.
2. You have the potential to earn a percentage of interest based on the performance of a market index or indices without ever being invested in the market. The particular indexes

used to determine your interest credits will be defined by the particular contract you may purchase and the interest-crediting strategies contained therein.

3. Most contracts lock in any interest credits at the end of each year on the contract's anniversary date. We call that an "earnings reset," but it is commonly referred to as an annual reset. Interest credits are generally subject to a cap or participation rate that will limit the amount of interest credited to your contract. An example would be if I purchased a fixed index annuity with $100,000 and allocated all of the premium to an indexed interest crediting strategy that had a 5% cap. On my anniversary lock-in date, the index performance over that year is measured and let's assume it had grown 8%. Because the strategy to which my money was allocated had a 5% cap, my contract is credited with 5% interest. The contract value of my annuity as of that date would then be $105,000. Had the index declined in value, my annuity would have received zero interest credits and the contract value would have remained the same.

4. Some contracts offer income riders (which are typically optional for an additional fee) that guarantee an enhanced income payout in retirement. The amount of income you receive is derived from the rider's benefit base. The benefit base is separate from the annuity's contract value and not an amount you can actually access in a lump sum; rather, it represents insurance proceeds earmarked specifically for your retirement income. The benefit base is typically credited with a fixed interest rate for a specified period of time. Your lifetime income benefit will then be calculated by multiplying the benefit base by a withdrawal percentage rate, such as 4 percent. If you opt for the benefit to pay out as long as both you and your spouse live, the percentage will be lower and will generally be based on the age of the younger spouse. The younger the spouse, the lower the withdrawal percentage.

5. Some income riders also feature a benefit that will waive surrender charges on income withdrawals made to help fund home health care, nursing home care and/or long-term care. This means that if you meet certain criteria — such as being unable to perform at least 2 of the 6 basic activities of daily living (ADL) — your annual withdrawal rate may increase for a specific number of years (e.g., 5 years) to help pay for additional infirmity expenses. So, if the contractual guaranteed income amount equals, say, $3,000 per month, but my doctor says I am unable to perform two ADLs such as dressing, walking feeding myself, moving from bed to chair, or am incontinent, or have severe cognitive impairment, my monthly income may double to $6,000 per month. After the specified time period or , your previous withdrawal rate will resume. This can be particularly helpful following an acute medical recovery period, such as a stroke, when you or your spouse needs assistance performing ADLs. Review the contract language to determine the length of the double income and the specifics for qualification.

One thing to always keep in mind is be cautious how much you use to purchase an annuity. You always want to leave other monies liquid where you can have access when needed. Annuities are longer-term strategies with limited liquidity. That is why there are some distinct advantages to using the right kind.

Fixed Index Annuities Go Up But Not DOWN

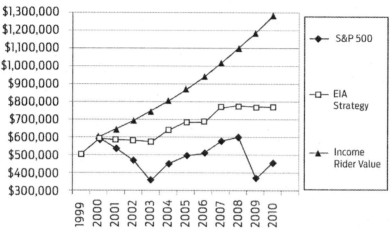

Eric's Story

In 2008, a few weeks after the financial crisis hit, I met a gentleman named Eric. He was in what we call the "retirement red zone," within five years of retirement. His goal was to be retired in three years.

Eric had saved $900,000, and his goal was to have $1 million in his market-based investment account by the time he retired. He told me he would need to withdraw $60,000 per year to cover his expenses.

If you have paid attention to the information that appeared in previous chapters, you would know the math just wasn't adding up for Eric. His projected income of $60,000 was way too much to withdraw per year without running out of money. Even in the economic climate the way it was before the crash, $40,000 would have been closer to an appropriate number.

When the financial crisis hit, he was paying a large brokerage firm to manage his retirement account, and his balance began to drop fast, just like the stock market. I told him we could run an analysis on the investments he was in and see if we could offer some recommendations. The analysis took three days to complete. By the time he came back in, the account was down to $820,000 and Eric was in a panic.

I meet with many people like Eric who have almost all their retirement money tied up at risk in the market. When I first mention the word "annuity" to them, people are quick to say they don't like them. But when we take the time to explore behind the clock face and see how they work to our advantage and where they can fit within the context of a larger portfolio, their value becomes apparent. After all, if we want a portion of our assets exempt from riding the ups and downs of the market, but we also don't want them sitting in a bank account losing ground to inflation, where else can we put them? It's quite the "aha" moment.

The Three Biggest Takeaways:

1. **Safe money:** Because this bucket could be considered protected principal money, it allows you to invest in the other buckets that are stock driven and possibly reduce your overall risk.
2. **Higher cash flow:** This bucket allows you to increase your cash flow so that you're not having to withdraw as much from your stock-driven buckets.
3. **Enhanced income:** With some of these products, a higher income may be paid for a limited number of months or years if long-term care is needed. This typically requires an authorization from your physician that you are unable to perform 2 activities of daily living or that you have a severe cognitive

impairment. Understand that higher income payments will accelerate the depreciation of your benefit base as well as the annuity's underlying contract value.

Action Item:

Don't buy an annuity until you understand the benefits and the limitations. They are not for everyone, but the right types of annuities can solve income needs and manage risk.

CHAPTER TEN

"Why Would I Need Life Insurance If I Am Approaching Retirement?"

I f I'm soon to be retired or already retired, why would I still need life insurance?

At this writing, I have been working with people for more than 26 years, helping them determine their insurance needs. I have met some folks who say they are "insurance poor" — an expression meaning they are over-insured. I have also met some families who needed all the life insurance they could possibly afford and qualify for.

Let me share some examples of where the right kind of life insurance could be an absolute financial life-saver.

The premature death of an income-earner. Losing a paycheck from the death of a loved one can be a life-changer. Financially, it can be catastrophic. Imagine that loss in your mind. Nothing can bring the loved one back, of course. But if the loved one left behind a legacy of financial security, that could make life better for those who survive. How much life insurance is needed? That depends on your income needs and your age.

Take the case of Dawn. Dawn was married to Brad, who was a hard worker and had been employed by the same company for 20 years. Brad had worked his way up the ladder and was bringing home a nice paycheck every month. Dawn didn't have to work outside the home. This allowed her to focus on raising their children, which she considered a full-time job.

Dawn and Brad were a team. It was Christmas Eve. Brad was visiting a neighbor, and was driving home when he was hit by a drunk driver in a head-on collision. Dawn and her family were devastated. How could this happen?

Fortunately, Brad had life insurance. The coverage was enough for Dawn to pay off all their debt and replace most of the income that was lost when Brad died. What would Dawn's life have been like without the life insurance? She would most likely have had to sell their home — a place that held so many memories for her — and move in with a family member. She would have had to find a job at a time when good jobs weren't available for someone with very little work experience. Dawn didn't have to make any of those decisions, thanks to the life insurance policy Brad had purchased years earlier.

Pension replacement. If you are one of the few people blessed with a pension, what happens to that pension when you die? If you chose life-only, or a "full" pension option, then the pension goes away. Even if you chose the survivorship option, it may be reduced up to 50 percent. What kind of impact would that loss of income have on your financial picture? How much interest and dividends would it take to replace that income?

If you have a spouse and you are both on Social Security, the smallest of the two checks goes away, too. That's two paychecks that could potentially disappear with the death of one spouse. How would you make up that loss of income? How large a nest egg would you need to have to compensate for that? Life insurance could fund that income replacement and you would have an income-tax-free bucket of money to draw from.

Lee was a self-investor. He loved playing with stocks. I am not opposed to self-investing, if that is a person's passion. As a matter of fact, I encourage it, and try to assist people who love to chart their own way through the Wall Street landscape. My only caution is not to risk assets they cannot afford to lose.

Lee needed some pointers on how to diversify his investments and manage his risk, but the main reason he sought the assistance of a financial advisor was because he had chosen a full-pension option when he retired from his employer to get the largest check he could. He knew that left his family vulnerable and recognized the need to be able to replace that income if he were to have died prematurely. So, he bought a life insurance policy. The problem was, he bought a term policy. According to the provisions of term life insurance, the premiums are locked in for the duration of the term. The younger you are, the lower the premiums. Your premiums may be relatively low for five, 10, or 20 years, but can sky rocket when the term runs out.

Buying term life insurance may be sufficient if you are using it to pay off a mortgage, and the term coincides with the expiration of the term. But when you are insuring a life, and the income generated by that person's life, term may not be the best option. Because of Lee's continued good health, he was able to find a permanent policy that gave him and his wife, Diane, a bit more protection than they had with the term life, all without a huge increase in his premiums.

What would have happened if Lee had died soon after the term policy ended? What would have happened if Lee had got the notification that his term coverage could be renewed, but only with a prohibitive rate increase? Diane would have been forced to spend down their nest egg. She could have ended up impoverished before she passed away. But, thanks to life insurance, those crises were avoided.

Accelerated benefit riders. Life insurance has changed in the last decade or so. It's become more creative. Insurance companies, like any other enterprise, are in business to make a profit. To continue to be profitable, they must cater to the consumers they serve. They must, therefore, keep up with the shifts in the economic landscape. Just like other corporations, insurance companies employ product design people who are continually scanning the horizon for areas where they can improve their offerings to be more competitive and appealing. Like many companies, they are eager to find a need and offer solutions to fill that need.

For years, life insurance was based on the straightforward idea that you pay a premium and your heirs receive a check when you die. *Accelerated benefit riders* are options tacked onto a policy that make it possible for policyholders, under certain circumstances, to enjoy benefits while they are still alive. These riders can greatly enhance the quality of life for those with terminal illnesses. No one likes thinking about such things, but, as you can imagine, obtaining medical care for a terminal illness can be quite expensive. Depending on the insurance company, these "living benefits" typically range from 25–100 percent of the policy's "face amount," or death benefit. After death, whatever is left over is paid to beneficiaries. With some policies, living benefit provisions are built into the policy, in which case the cost is built into the premium. In other cases, they appear as riders, are optional, and cost extra.

Several conditions could trigger payment of a living benefit:

- Contracting an illness that is expected to result in your death within two years.
- Contracting an illness that a physician certifies will reduce your lifespan
- Contracting an illness that will result in an organ transplant
- Inability to perform ADLs (activities of daily living), such as bathing by yourself or feeding yourself
- Entering hospice (end-of-life care).

What happens if you recover from your illness? Most contracts do not require you to repay the benefits, but the death benefit is reduced by the amount paid out. Let's say you bought a life insurance policy with a $500,000 death benefit, and your policy has a chronic illness rider. There's the money to fund long-term-care expenses. What if it turns out that long-term care does not prove necessary? Then your beneficiary (or beneficiaries) inherit the $500,000, tax-free. Remember, every policy is different, so you need to read and understand the provisions.

Tax-free income. Did your eyebrows just arch a little, and your ears perk up? Yes, life insurance policies exist nowadays that can, *if properly structured*, provide *tax-free income* to policyowners. More and more Americans are using this strategy to augment their cash flow in retirement.

Just so you will understand this type of insurance more fully, allow me to start at the beginning. There was an insurance revolution of sorts in the early 1980s. Remember in Chapter One of this book, we talked about inflation and the effect it had on the nation in the late 1970s and early 1980s? If you are a baby boomer, you probably remember the days back when Jimmy

Carter was president and inflation was spiraling out of control. As we mentioned, it wasn't Carter's fault. He inherited the whirlwind caused by his predecessors' attempts to control inflation by wage and price control. This over-regulation of the economy sparked double-digit interest rates and wild-fire inflation just about the time early baby boomers were coming of age financially. They were starting families. They were buying homes, cars and, oh yes, *life insurance* to protect their families.

But insurance had not kept up with the times. Financially speaking, they were stuck in the 1950s. In the 1970s, traditional whole life policies were paying a paltry 1 or 2 percent interest on the cash-value portion of their contracts, while down at the local bank you could get double-digit interest on a savings account! People began cashing in whole life policies by the thousands, opting for cheaper term policies for the protection element and investing their money elsewhere where it would at least keep up with inflation. "Buy term and invest the difference" was an insurance concept that began sweeping the nation, and insurance companies were forced to reinvent themselves.

Insurance companies got their actuaries and product design people together and asked them to come up with a solution. The result was something new called "universal life insurance," or UL for short. The concept was all about flexibility and transparency. Interest paid on the cash value portion of these new policies would no longer be an arbitrary one or two percent, but would be based on what U.S. Treasury bills were yielding, which in 1982 was 14.59 percent![21]

Policyholders could now track their returns by checking the newspaper or calling the insurance company. Premiums were flexible. You could accelerate the cash value by overpaying premiums if you wished, or you could pay the minimum – just

---

[21] MULTPL. Jan. 1, 2018. "10 Year Treasury Rate by Year." http://www.multpl.com/10-year-treasury-rate/table/by-year.

enough to cover the death benefit. If your policy had accumulated cash, you could even skip premiums and let your cash value pay them for you. Death benefits were still tax-free to beneficiaries, and policyholders could make withdrawals from the cash value in the form of low-interest loans.

With these changes, it wasn't long before universal life began to gain back some of the ground it had lost to the "buy-term-and-invest-the-difference" movement. With inflation pressures subsiding, interest rates eventually came off their double-digit peaks. The prime rate dropped from 10.87 percent in 1989 to 6 percent in 1994. The drop in T-bills diminished some of the appeal of UL policies, so it was back to the drawing board for insurance companies.

Indexed universal life was introduced in 1997. This new concept pegged interest on cash value to the upward movement of a stock-market index, such as the S&P 500 — thus the term. Indexed universal life retained the desirable characteristics of premium flexibility and adjustable face value (death benefit), and continued to allow policyowners to "overfund," or pour more premium dollars into the policy than was needed to cover the cost of the death benefit for the purpose of accelerating cash growth. Now people could benefit from a surging stock market without being negatively affected by its downside since premium dollars are never actually invested in the market.

There were some glitches that had to be worked out, however. When these policies first came out, people could pump as much as they wished into these policies. So, what's wrong with that? Nothing, as far as the policyowner was concerned. The cash value grew tax-deferred and could be removed tax-free. But Uncle Sam wasn't too pleased with the arrangement, and soon plugged the loophole with new laws that would limit the amount you could put in these policies. The new laws soon came to be known by their acronyms, TEFRA, DEFRA and TAMRA.

- TEFRA: Tax, Equity, Fiscal and Responsibility Act of 1982.
- DEFRA: Deficit Reduction Act of 1984.
- TAMRA: Technical and Miscellaneous Revenue Act of 1988.

In one way or another, these regulations curbed abuse of the tax-free provisions of indexed universal life, but left the provisions intact that allowed policies to benefit from the upward movement of the stock market while not participating in its losses.

How does the tax-free income part of IUL work? The cash value inside the policy grows tax-deferred and, if designed properly, it can be pulled out as tax-free loans that don't have to be paid back during the insured's life. The insurance company uses some of the death benefit to pay off the loan.

This strategy can be an excellent way to plan for additional cash flow in retirement, and the tax-free element is huge. Some higher income-earners aren't eligible to contribute to Roth IRAs, so pulling a steady tax-free stream of income from their life insurance policy is their alternative strategy.

Once, when I was hosting my radio show, "Financial Symphony," a physician called in and said he was 50 years old and needed life insurance to protect his family. While we were on the air, I briefly shared with him some of the options available to him. During the next break, we discussed his needs and his goals. He was a high income-earner and knew how beneficial a monthly tax-free check at retirement would be as part of his overall income plan. I didn't have to elaborate on the benefits of lessening his tax burden. Since his annual income exceeded the limits placed by the government on Roth IRA contributions, this solution was a win/win for him and his family. He had the death benefit to take care of his wife and children in the event he prematurely lost his life, and all those premiums he would be paying through the years would be growing inside the policy. That growth would later be used as a source of tax-free income.

Offsetting tax burdens. When your children inherit your traditional IRAs and 401(k)s, they also inherit a tax bill. Right now, there are trillions of dollars in these savings accounts that have never been taxed. Uncle Sam is just sitting there, patiently waiting for the withdrawals to start so he can get a slice of that pie, or for the owners of the accounts to die and leave them in a lump sum to their beneficiaries, when he will get an even bigger slice.

The Investment Company Institute, an investment industry research organization, released statistics stating, as of June 22, 2017, assets in individual retirement accounts (IRAs) totaled $8.2 trillion at the end of the first quarter of 2017, an increase of 4.1 percent from the previous year. As of Sept. 27, 2017, the ICI puts the total retirement assets of the country at $26.6 trillion. Retirement assets account for 36 percent of all household financial assets in the United States.[22]

That's not necessarily bad news. But almost all that money, once it is withdrawn or passed along to beneficiaries, will immediately create a looming tax problem. In fact, we call these accounts "ticking tax time bombs." I can't take credit for that phrase. It was coined by CPA and New York Times best-selling author Ed Slott when he wrote his 2003 book, "The Retirement Savings Time Bomb and How to Diffuse It."

"With the possible exception of home property, the most valuable asset for Americans is their retirement fund," Slott points out in his book. "Yet, most people don't know how to avoid the costly mistakes that cause a good chunk of those savings to be lost to needless and excessive taxation."

That is so true. When people retire, many of them discover the money in these qualified accounts represent their means of

---

[22] Investment Company Institute. 2017. "Retirement Research." https://www.ici.org/research/retirement.

survival for the next 20-30 years. It is downright painful, then, when a big chunk of it must be paid out to Uncle Sam. Do not be shocked if Congress changes the rules to tax an inherited IRA more quickly than it presently does.

And let me ask you a question. With trillions of dollars of national debt in place as this book is written, do you think taxes will increase or decrease in the future? If you answered increase, please go to the head of the class. This is why many feel it makes sense to spend your IRAs during retirement while we are seeing some of the lowest tax brackets in history. But wait a minute! What about our children and grandchildren? That's where life insurance and its tax-free death benefit comes in. If we spend our taxable money now and leave life insurance to heirs, we have adjusted taxes in our favor and eliminated a tax burden on the loved ones we leave behind.

Beth came into my office to invest her retirement. She had two life insurance policies she had bought several years before.

She said, "Mark, I want to spend my retirement accounts while I'm alive, and these two policies are for my children." She had a plan in place, she needed a second opinion and some help with investing efficiently. Wise woman. I am very proud of her.

I was filling up my tank at a gas station off Interstate 85 recently, where I spotted on the back of a very nice motor home a bumper sticker that read: "We are spending our children's inheritance." I struck up a conversation with the driver of the RV, a man who appeared to be in his early 70s, about the bumper sticker.

"I know how it sounds," he said with a laugh, "but believe me, the kids don't need our money. The son is a doctor, and the daughter gets a big salary as CEO of a large corporation."

I learned the driver of the motor home had worked hard all his life to grow a successful construction business in Massachusetts, and his wife had been a teacher. They were the same age and had retired at 63. He told me he had bought as much life insurance as he could qualify for when he was in his 40s, and I commended him for his foresight.

"We are on our way to see Mount Rushmore," he said. "I've always wanted to see the place. I would like to spend every penny and have the last check bounce."

I doubt if the man had ever written a bad check in his life, but I knew what he meant. The most successful retirement plan ever devised is one where you can enjoy life to the fullest in your golden years while knowing your loved ones will be well cared for when you "shuffle off this mortal coil."

Action Item:

Work with an insurance professional you trust to explain the benefits and limitations clearly so you can understand what each policy can do for your situation.

CHAPTER ELEVEN

This Ain't Your Daddy's Retirement!

The new Mercedes Benz Stadium in Atlanta, Georgia, is home to the Atlanta Falcons who *almost* won the 2017 Super Bowl and seats 75,000 people. That's a lot of folks. If you can get a mental picture of that stadium packed to capacity, and then imagine that many people retiring in a single week, you can get an idea of the enormous impact retiring baby boomers are having on the nation and its economy.

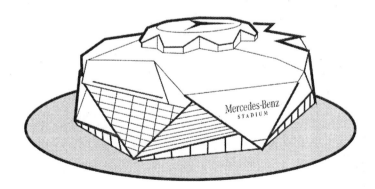

As I mentioned in Chapter Eight, the way people retire these days is completely different than it was decades ago. Times were when you worked for a company or corporation for 25 or 30 years, and they would give you a nice gold watch and a pension for life. These days, pensions are rare as ducks with hats.

Think about it — there was a time in America when it was much easier to retire with confidence that our financial future would not be endangered by running out of money. We had Social Security. Most people had no doubt it would be there for them when they reached retirement. They had confidence when they turned in their notice to the boss and severed their umbilical paychecks, they could cruise into their golden years with a guaranteed source of income. Decades ago, one could deposit money at the bank in money markets and actually expect a good rate of return. Bank CDs were not a joke. When it came to stocks, you could invest in blue chips (big U.S. companies) and sit back and receive dividends. My, how times have changed.

Social Security has changed. You must work longer to get full Social Security. Full retirement age used to be **65.** As this book is written, you can claim early retirement at age 62, but the caveat is a 25 percent reduction to your full benefit amount. The current full benefit age is 66 for people born between 1943 and 1954. It will gradually rise to 67 for those born after 1960.[23]

Many American workers are unsure if it will even be there for them when they retire. Even the Social Security Administration acknowledges, unless changes are made, the program as we now know it will not be available for retirees decades hence.

Here's a stark warning from the SSA's annual Trustee's Report of 2014:

> "Social Security is not sustainable over the long term at current benefit and tax rates. In 2010, the program paid more in

---

[23] Social Security. 2017. "Retirement Planner: Full Retirement Age." https://www.ssa.gov/planners/retire/retirechart.html.

benefits and expenses than it collected in taxes and other non-interest income, and the 2014 Trustees Report projects this pattern to continue for the next 75 years."[24]

Not too long ago, a client handed me a copy of his Social Security statement and pointed out the following dire warning that appeared on its front page.

About Social Security's Future:

"Social Security is a compact between generations. Since 1935, America has kept the promise of security for its workers and their families. Now, however, the Social Security system is facing serious financial problems, and action is needed soon to make sure the system will be sound when today's younger workers are ready for retirement.

"Without changes, in 2033 the Social Security Trust Fund will be able to pay only about 77 cents for each dollar of scheduled benefits. We need to resolve these issues soon to make sure Social Security continues to provide a foundation of protection for future generations."

I think this is why some people are in such a rush to collect their benefits as soon as they become eligible, usually at age 62. They want to get what is owed them before the program disappears. But before you press the panic button, folks, notice that even the SSA trustees calculate the program will continue as-is until 2033. Changes will likely either extend retirement age, increase the amount contributed by workers, reduce benefits or a combination of all of the above. Of course, anything could happen, but it is unlikely that Social Security will not be there for baby boomers when they retire.

---

[24] Social Security. 2014. "2014 OASDI Trustees Report." https://www.ssa.gov/oact/tr/2014/index.html.

Download Your Statement

If you haven't read over your Social Security statement in a while, it may be worth your while to check it out. It will show your earnings record and your estimated Social Security payments at full retirement age, as well as how much you will receive if you take it early or wait until you are age 70. Times were when you received a paper copy in the mail. To cut costs, the Social Security Administration is now directing you to their website, www.SSA.gov, where you may set up a "My Social Security" account.

Once you have established your account with the SSA, you can check to make sure the government has your correct earnings going back to when you first began receiving paychecks. Why is that important? Because the government calculates your benefits based on your highest 35 years of earnings. If an error has been made on your earnings history, it could significantly affect your retirement benefits.

Changing Retirement Landscape.

The retirement landscape in America has changed much since yesteryear. Back in the 1930s, when Franklin Delano Roosevelt was elected president, wages were low and jobs were scarce, but part of the New Deal FDR promoted was a promise that workers could expect both Social Security and a pension when they retired. Two generations of Americans came up under that arrangement. If you worked for a large company, you had a lifetime income to help you pay your bills. With workers' pensions virtually a thing of the past, what's left as income sources are Social Security, 401(k)/IRA and similar programs, and your personal savings.

Contemplate what you have in your sources of income. Is it enough to serve as a pension for the rest of your life in retirement, which could last 30 years or longer? Chicago Tribune reporter Gail MarksJarvis observes many baby boomers are deciding to work past the typical retirement age of 65 because they have not saved enough. Picture that. Millions of 70-somethings trying to squeeze into an already-crowded labor market in a last-gasp effort to fill their retirement hope chests. MarksJarvis predicts that, as time goes by, older workers will settle for lower wages in the scramble for jobs. She writes, "The Bureau of Labor Statistics has estimated that 7.2 million people over 55 will be in the labor force in 2024. That group of older workers is expected to be the fastest-growing part of the labor force."[25]

Retirement should be a time of rest, relaxation and finally doing all the things you couldn't do when you were working. But for those who have done inadequate retirement income planning, retirement can be downright frightening. When it comes to retirement strategies, what worked for the parents of boomers won't work in the 21st century. An example is the now debunked "4 Percent Withdrawal Rule," which I covered in Chapter Five. People retiring in the decades of the 1980s and 1990s were told they could remove 4 percent per year from their portfolio, rebalance it annually, and their money would last as long as they did. After the financial crisis of 2008 and the ensuing Great Recession, coupled with the subsequent sideways performance of the stock market, you don't hear much about the "4 Percent Rule" anymore.

For those whose income-producing portfolios are not truly diversified, they may find themselves at the mercy of a stock market subject to extreme volatility and wild fluctuations. Why?

---

[25] Gail MarksJarvis. Chicago Tribune. June 3, 2017. "Baby Boomers Planning to Work Past Retirement? Here's Why that Idea Could Be a Bust." http://www.chicagotribune.com/business/columnists/ct-baby-boomer-retirement-rescue-trouble-column-marksjarvis-0604-biz-20170601-column.html.

Because we live in a world where what happens on one side of the globe is reported within seconds on the other side. The news is on 24 hours a day, seven days a week, and virtually anything can happen. These events can fuel knee-jerk reactions by traders and cause ripple effects across the world. If you are in the unfortunate position of having to live off the income from investments that can be so easily threatened, you will naturally experience much stress and many sleepless nights. These are scary times to be a do-it-yourself investor headed for retirement. Any mistake could be catastrophic.

What about 401(k)s? Aren't they immune from such losses? After all, aren't they controlled by professional investors who know what they are doing? Not really. According to the Employee Benefit Research institute (EBRI), "During 2008, major U.S. equity indexes were sharply negative, with the S&P 500 Index losing 37 percent for the year, which translated into corresponding losses in 401(k) retirement plan assets."[26]

That may not have been disastrous for younger workers. They had time on their side and could wait for the market to rebound and make up their losses. But for workers who were at the cusp of retirement, their life's savings were nonrenewable resources. They were hurt badly. Defined-contribution plans (like 401(k)s) are great vehicles for helping workers save for retirement. But the funds within these programs are invested primarily in mutual funds where there are no guarantees. Investment choices are ultimately up to the employees themselves. That means, if they invest unwisely, they could lose a significant portion of what they worked so hard to save, and just when they need it most.

---

[26] EBRI. February 2009. "The Impact of the Recent Financial Crisis on 401(k) Account Balances." https://www.ebri.org/publications/ib/?fa=ibDisp&content_id=4192.

Robot Investment Advice

I have to hand it to technology. I have benefited from and enjoy using a smartphone, and I visit the neighborhood ATM on occasion. I, too, have become dependent on email as a form of communication, and I am slowly warming up to the idea that cars can safely drive themselves. But one phenomenon I did not think I would live to see, and am having a difficult time seeing the merit of, is a disembodied computer program preparing you for retirement.

Automated investing, or "robo-investing," as it has been dubbed, is becoming more and more popular these days. Commercials aimed at DIY investors promise to make the process effortless and easy through technology. "Put your investing on autopilot," promises one spot. If you buy their software, you can "invest like a professional" and "put technology to work for you." The commercials promise to "build a personal portfolio for you in just five minutes that will put your money to work like the world's smartest investors."

Why do I have flashbacks to the old black and white "Lost in Space" episodes, with the robot waving his pincers saying, "Danger, danger, Will Robinson!"

The commercials make it sound so easy, don't they? And perhaps there are some formulaic recipes for informal trading and portfolio rebalancing that may work for the do-it-yourself stock trader, but no robot can sort through the complexities of retirement income planning. There are just too many variables. First of all, no two people are alike. Retirement planning calls for tailor-made strategies based on individual financial situations. They are not capable of guiding you through life changes that require adjustments in your plan. There is simply no way to replace the human element of analysis, sensitivity and understanding that a living, breathing human brings to the table.

Sometimes, we the investor become the problem. We make the same classic mistakes over and over again. That's just one of the reasons I say, "This ain't your father's retirement."

Replacing Pensions

What if you could guarantee yourself a lifetime income just like the old pension plans of your parent's generation? That's what many baby boomers are doing.

There's something out there these days known as the LIA — longevity income annuity. In 2014, the U.S. Treasury Department issued rules designed to add pension-like characteristics to 401(k) programs. The new rules make it easier to convert funds from retirement savings, such as the 401(k), into a type of annuity that guarantees an income stream in your golden years.

A report produced in 2016 by the National Bureau of Economic Research calls it "putting the pension back in 401(k) plans."

"Most defined-contribution pension plans pay benefits as lump sums," says the NBER report, "yet the U.S. Treasury has recently encouraged firms to protect retirees from outliving their assets by converting a portion of their plan balances into longevity income annuities (LIA). These are deferred annuities that initiate payouts not later than age 85 and continue for life."

The NBER describes LIAs as a relatively inexpensive way to allow people to hedge longevity risk. The idea is to use a small portion of your retirement account balance at retirement to purchase an LIA, which would then pay you an income for life at a later date. Suppose you are 65, and you have $100,000 your 401(k). You could buy an LIA for $10,000, which would begin paying you around $4,000 per year from age 85 onward. That's an approximate figure because it is impacted by the interest-rate environment and whether you are male or female.[27]

LIAs aren't for everyone, and some will benefit from them more than others. Individuals whose retirement savings are more substantial may be better served by looking into other products that are designed to produce a lifetime income stream, such as fixed index annuities that link their interest earnings to the growth of the stock market but do not participate in its losses. Annuities are contracts between an insurance company and an individual, so it is important to understand them thoroughly before you sign anything, and consult a financial professional who is a fiduciary and can help you decide if such a contract is best for you.

---

[27] National Bureau of Economic Research. October 2016. "Putting the Pension Back in 401(k) Plans: Optimal versus Default Longevity Income Annuities." http://www.nber.org/papers/w22717.

Seeking Professional Help

In England, where winters can be damp and dreary, Terry Southerton, a 21-year-old mother, desperately wanted a suntan. She wanted to look like the women she saw strolling on the beaches in the pictures she saw in glamor magazines. Since the sun would not cooperate, Terri decided to search the internet for an alternative solution. She came across an advertisement for a tanning chemical called Melanotan. The ad promised if she injected herself with 3 milligrams of this substance, her skin would take on a coppery shade within a few hours, making her look like she had spent a week on Caribbean beaches. She sent off for it, but, as you may have guessed, things didn't turn out well for Terri.

"Looking back, I can't believe I was so stupid," she told a reporter for the Daily Mail, a London tabloid newspaper that reported the incident. "I didn't see any effects until two days after the injection. Then bizarre things started to happen. My face became luminous and swollen. I had the strangest green tinge and became hypersensitive. It was itchy, painful and I couldn't bear to touch it."

The woman survived, but she learned a lesson about the dangers of injecting herself with substances purchased through the internet.[28]

Just as no rational person would consider self-surgery or self-dentistry, the same principle should apply to do-it-yourself financial planning. It's not that you *can't* do it. Certainly not all DIY financial planning efforts end up in disaster. But I have spent decades in the financial advisory profession, and I heard about and personally witnessed many amateur mistakes that have cost do-it-yourselfers thousands of dollars in needless losses, both in unrealized gains and unnecessary taxes. In just about every case, the mistakes they made could have been avoided. All this has led me to believe — my own bias notwithstanding — it is wise to trust managing your wealth to professionals, the same way you would trust managing your health to those who are fully trained and oath-bound to protect it.

One man I know used to boast that he had no need of doctors.

"I haven't seen a doctor in 30 years," he told me. He was telling the truth, too. With the exception of an occasional sniffle, he had never been sick. He looked in great shape and was very physically active. The only medicine he took was an occasional aspirin for a headache. That's why it came as a shock to his family and friends when he dropped dead suddenly of a massive heart attack. Who knew his blood pressure and cholesterol numbers were off the charts, and that he was a walking myocardial infarction waiting to happen? No one. He might still be alive if he had at least gone in for the occasional checkup — you know, the kind that always starts with a blood pressure check.

---

[28] John Naish. Daily Mail. April 28, 2011. "The Deadly Tan Job." http://www.dailymail.co.uk/femail/article-1381298/The-deadly-tan-jab-DIY-injection-promising-instant-tan-women-discovered-trigger-heart-disease-cancer.html.

Finding Good Financial Advice

First of all, let's talk about the places you probably won't get good financial advice. Please don't laugh when you read this. I wish I had a dollar for every thousand lost by people who have staked their financial fortunes on advice received from the following sources:

- **Well-meaning family members.** Good old Uncle Harry at the family reunion. He probably means well when he gives you the stock tip of the century, but don't bet your retirement income on it.
- **The office coffee room, neighborhood bar or beauty salon.** Believe it or not, some have staked their financial future on conversations heard or overheard at such places. Remember, friends don't let friends take financial advice from casual conversations around the office water cooler.
- **The internet.** It is true you can find just about anything you are looking for on the internet — including financial advice. Yet, for every expert opinion you find on the internet, you can find another one pointing you in the opposite direction.
- **Your favorite bank teller.** The people at your local bank can be very friendly. They know you by your first name. But unless they are an Investment Advisor Representative or a Certified Financial Planner™, they probably don't have the licensure or credentials to educate you about a comprehensive financial plan. But you would be surprised to know how many people entrust their financial futures to these friendly faces behind the marble counters of their local banks.

On airplane emergency exit doors, you will see in large, red letters, "Do Not Open While in Flight." You would think this warning is unnecessary. But, the warning probably wouldn't be there if, at some point in the past, someone hadn't attempted to do just that. I have heard horror stories about retirements that met with disaster because of well-meaning but untrustworthy advice volunteered by trusted but unqualified friends or relatives.

So, what should you do?

Work with a licensed professional and ask lots of questions. Remember, the financial advisor you select works for *you*. Interview him or her as if you were a business owner hiring a manager. You want someone you can trust, and you want an individual with the proper credentials, education and experience. You also want an individual — and this is critical — who is on the same page philosophically who can understand your vision of the future and help you reach your goals. You want *your* agenda to dominate the end result — not that of the financial professional.

What kind of questions should you ask?

How are you paid? In polite society, asking someone how (or how much) they are compensated may be considered rudeness. But. to quote a line from "The Godfather," this isn't personal, it's business. You aren't asking about the financial professional's personal life; you want to know if there is a possible conflict of interest. For example, Investment Advisor Representatives usually work on a fee-only or a fee-plus-commission basis. With fee-only compensation arrangements, the advisor charges either flat fees or hourly fees (somewhat like an attorney). Many investment advisor representatives charge a percentage of the assets you have under management with them. Industry standards are usually 1–2 percent. This rewards the advisor for growing your portfolio. The flat fees or hourly charges usually come with a one-time service, such developing a financial plan or structuring an estate plan. The fee may vary according to the amount of service rendered or the size of the accounts involved.

Do you make a commission? Commission is not a dirty word. Think of a travel agent. When you hire a travel agency to plan a trip for you, what is their job? (a) To save you money on fares, hotel bills, etc. and (b) to enhance your travel experience. What does it cost you? Nothing! The job of the travel agent is to find out where you are going, what you want to do there, and determine your budget. The agent pulls together the best fares and most efficient travel schedule. Only then does the travel agent create your itinerary. How is the travel agent compensated? By commissions from the vendors. Does it offend you if the airlines or hotels pay the agent commission? Of course not! It doesn't come out of your pocket. In fact, if the travel agent knows what he is doing, it should put money *in* your pocket. If you had to do the work yourself, you would probably not possess the skills to make it all happen. You might even make a mess of it!

What is your approach to investing? This is a trick question, especially if you ask it on the initial interview. Why? Because the financial advisor who has your interests at heart will adjust his approach to investing to suit your financial needs and your goals for retirement. The answer to that question can only be given after hearing the answers to several questions about where you are financially and where you want to go. A true fiduciary financial advisor will have to first gauge your risk tolerance, your estate plans, your tax situation and your retirement timetable. You probably wouldn't have much confidence in a doctor who prescribed medicine without first asking what other medications you were taking and any allergies you may have. The same principle applies to handing out cookie-cutter financial advice without first having a clear understanding of the client's financial situation.

Are you a fiduciary? We covered what a fiduciary is in Chapter Six, but it's worth repeating here in the list of questions you should ask a financial advisor candidate. If the answer is no, or if you have to explain what a fiduciary is, you are probably in the wrong place.

How will we work together long-term? You should have a good idea of what will characterize your relationship with your financial advisory firm. Who will be your contact person at the firm when you have a question to ask about your portfolio? You simply must have good communication between your advisor and you. Who will your designated contact person be when you call the office to ask a question? Will you have access to the firm's principals in the future if you need them? How often will your financial plan be reviewed? Who are the other members of your professional team? What role do each of them play?

What are your credentials? True professionals will welcome this question. They will be pleased to tell you about their training, experience and certifications. You may find this information on the walls of their office or on their business card, but not always. You can't always judge competency by letters after a name on a business card, but it is perfectly OK to ask what they stand for. There are nearly as many designations and certifications for financial advisors as there are letters in the alphabet. Many of them are variations on the same theme, and some of them are redundant, but the following glossary may help:

CIMA® (Certified Investment Management Analysts) CIMAs focus on asset allocation and typically complete final coursework at the Haas School of Business at the University of California, Berkeley, or at the University of Pennsylvania's Wharton School of Business.

CFP® (CERTIFIED FINANCIAL PLANNER™) CFPs have completed university-level financial planning coursework and passed a 10-hour exam covering nearly 90 topics, from group medical insurance to derivatives.

CFA® (CHARTERED FINANCIAL ANALYST®) CFAs must pass three exams, each of which demands a minimum of 250 hours of study and includes corporate finance and financial statements.

ChFC® (Chartered Financial Consultant) The ChFC® designation was introduced in 1982 as an alternative to the CFP®. It has the same core curriculum as CFP® plus a couple additional courses, but does not require a comprehensive board exam.

PFS (Personal Financial Specialist) PFSs are certified public accountants who specialize in personal financial planning. The credential requires a detailed exam and significant financial planning experience.

RFC (Registered Financial Consultant) This is a professional designation awarded by the International Association of Registered Financial Consultants (IARFC) to financial advisors who meet the high standards of education, experience and integrity required of all its members.

A Word of Caution

You need to know that some who hang out their shingle as a financial advisor are merely stockbrokers. Beverly, a 63-year-old widow, visited the office of a financial advisory firm in a large glass tower building. She had just received a sizable death benefit from a life insurance company and wanted to know how she should invest it. Aside from a few thousand dollars she and her husband had managed to save, the death benefit from the life insurance policy represented all the money she owned. What she needed at her age was a comprehensive retirement plan and a guaranteed lifetime income. What she received was a menu of investment choices of risky, riskier and riskiest.

"They showed me a pie chart with combinations of mutual funds, large and small cap stocks, international stocks and growth stocks and told me that this made my portfolio diversified," Beverly said. She was asked no questions about long-term care, taxes or estate planning. Why? Because she was talking to accumulation advisors, not retirement income advisors. There is a huge difference.

Another factor that cannot be defined by plaques on the wall or letters on a business card is experience. There is no substitute for a positive track record. It is the very foundation of trustworthiness. One can possess all the education in the world but lack character, and it is all for naught. The bond of trust you will build with your financial advisor over time is of inestimable value and is irreplaceable.

Regardless of whom you choose as your advisor, it is your financial journey and you must take charge of it. You are the captain of your ship. Your advisor is there to help you navigate the shoals and avoid the dangers. Your advisor's role is to coach and guide you. Of course, you must be coachable for this partnership to work.

One client we will call Rose was intelligent, but not very coachable. She went against my advice and recommendations. I met her and her husband through a referral from another client. They needed help on how to invest their nest egg. About a year into our professional relationship, two tragic developments occurred: She lost her job in a recession and her husband died. She had lost her salary and one of the two Social Security checks that she was counting on to make ends meet. Her budget changed little after her husband's death. Fortunately, the couple had managed to save a few hundred thousand dollars, but now she was forced to live off what was now for the most part a nonrenewable resource. Rose was at a financial crossroads and in dire need of financial direction, but was reluctant to accept it in any form. She began making one bad decision after another.

Her spending began to spiral out of control. Impulse-buying became a daily pattern. She took trips she couldn't afford and made inadvisable purchases that endangered her financial security. A daughter from a previous marriage wanted a condo, so Rose bought it for her. A couple of years later, the daughter moved out, leaving Rose with the property for which she had no use and did not know how to unload. As her financial advisor, I felt duty-bound to caution her about her spending and other financial decisions, but she would near none of it. She politely told me she would do as she wished, and that it made her feel good.

I do understand. Spending money can have a narcotic effect. It can be the opiate that soothes depression and brightens one's mood. I was looking down the road for her, however. My pleadings had to do with where she would be five years hence, when the money ran out. I knew the alarm bells would eventually sound, but by the time they did, her options would be severely limited. I felt like a doctor whose patient's well-being was being slowly eroded by overeating, but would not accept dietary advice. All I could do was join the family in watching her assets dwindle.

When Rose died, she had $11,000 to her name. I remember her well, but not for the best of reasons to remember a client — the one who would not follow advice.

A Simple Question

Barry asked me a simple question one day. "Why should I use your firm instead of XYZ?" (He mentioned the name of a large firm that advertises on TV and has millions of clients.)

The answer I gave him was simple, too. You may just be a number to them instead of a person with your own unique financial situation. Another reason is the big firms have a lot of turnover. I don't think you would like the idea of having to get acquainted with new advisors, telling them your story all over again each time you needed help from your firm.

I confess, I am not a big fan of some of the large financial advisory firms. Try this exercise: Google the name of a large firm you may be working with, and then type in "revenue-sharing disclosure" into the search engine. You will find a laundry list of mutual funds that are paying that firm to sell (push) their funds. You may even see the amounts these fund companies are paying the financial advisory firms. Does that smell a little fishy to you? Could there possibly be a conflict of interest there? You bet! If the firm giving you investment advice could possibly make more profit by using ABC mutual fund over XYZ mutual fund, that does not pass the sniff test of unbiased financial advice and is hardly how a true fiduciary relationship should work in an advisor/client relationship.

Here are some other considerations that should be on your mind when choosing the right financial advisor. Will they:

- Perform a stress test on your existing accounts to measure the risk you are taking versus the growth you are receiving? Will they assess if that risk matches your comfort level and is right for your retirement time horizon?
- Provide an income plan that includes budgeting your expenses and factoring in inflation?
- Help you optimize your Social Security benefit?
- Structure your income to be tax-efficient while you are living, and minimize tax liability for your heirs?
- Show you how to make your assets last for the duration of your retirement, regardless of how long you live?
- Educate you about how to efficiently pass your estate to your heirs with efficiency and as little interference as possible?
- Show you options and strategies that will protect your nest egg from future health care expenses?
- Provide proof that their returns are audited by a third party?

The Value of a Second Opinion

What is the value of a second opinion? When a patient is diagnosed with a serious illness requiring dangerous surgery, it is usually wise to get a second opinion. Two doctors, each with certification and training, may offer diametrically opposed opinions as to how to approach a cure. One may be conservative and another aggressive. One may recommend a traditional approach, while another may lean toward newer approaches.

When it comes to financial planning, you may not recognize you need a guide until you experience a wrong turn, like the one experienced by the aforementioned couple who sat in my office, asking for what amounted to directions on their financial journey. To avoid getting lost in the maze of financial planning and money management, the guide you choose must be able to give you clear and correct advice. But whom can we trust? Trust plays a significant role in making such a selection. That is why many gravitate to their friends or relatives for advice. Their advice is invalid, but it comes from a place of trust. One reason trust is such an issue these days is because there are so many differing opinions held by those who claim expertise in this area.

In the arena of financial advice, some advisors are polarized in their opinions. Some insist the only way to save, invest and plan for the future is by investing in mutual funds. Another advisor may insist insurance products, such as annuities and life insurance, are the only way. There is usually a reason for this type of myopia and one-sided advice — commissions. Personally, I view that as like a doctor prescribing medicine for patients in return for a kickback. Shame on that doctor for such unprofessional behavior! I believe such things are rare, but I have heard too many stories to think it does not exist.

Does greed motivate nonfiduciaries in the financial advisory profession? It can. But usually polarized opinions are more likely to spring from one's training, not avarice. Just as the medical profession has its die-hard adherents to a particular method of treatment, so do some financial advisors. They are zealots for a school of thought, probably because that's all they know. Can there be opposing schools of thought as to how to acquire and manage wealth and neither be wrong? Absolutely! And sometimes a combination of those two approaches can work quite well.

A friend of mine had terrible back pain and complained about it often.

"How's your back today?" I asked him, and he told me it was much better. When I asked him what he did to help it, he told me he finally decided to seek professional help.

"I went to my family doctor," he said, "and he told me to take muscle relaxers. Next, I went to my chiropractor, and she told me to come in for an adjustment."

"So, which one worked?" I asked.

"I guess they both did," he said. "I took the pills and got an adjustment. All I know, my back doesn't hurt anymore."

That makes an interesting point, doesn't it? Two professionals with two differing views and methods of treatment, both of which had some validity. If you got them both in the same room, however, they would probably square off over which treatment had more validity. Because of their training and experience, one advisor may recommend the use of equities for every solution, while another may advise the polar opposite.

In both life and money matters, sometimes opposing points of view are neither right nor wrong, and the truth (or what works) is often situated in the sizable middle ground between them. Professional points of view can be like that. What do you see when you look at this image? It is an optical illusion, of course, but do you see the profiles of two human faces, or a vase? Our perception of something can be limited by our viewpoint. So, which is it? A vase or a couple of faces? It's both.

Somewhere in my garage, I have a large, battered metal tool box that has to be 40 years old. I am no handyman, but I have accumulated a variety of tools over the years, mainly from home-repair projects and trips to the hardware store. Here is a truth about tools: every tool has its purpose. A hammer is no good for turning a screw, and a screwdriver makes a lousy hammer. But both are useful in their own right. Acquiring and preserving wealth and using it to forge a lifetime income for retirement requires several financial tools. It may include a mix of investments and strategies to get the job done. Some financial advisors may not be licensed to use certain tools. They may be securities licensed, but do not have permission from annuity carriers to offer their products. Some may be insurance licensed, but cannot offer market-based solutions. In my opinion, this is why a fiduciary advisor who is licensed and trained in multiple disciplines is better equipped to help you accomplish a carefree retirement. Getting a second opinion from a fiduciary advisor may help you prevent a serious miscalculation at this stage of the game — one that can cost you dearly.

Avoiding Miscalculations in the Retirement Red Zone

As mentioned in Chapter Two of this book, in football, the "red zone" is the area of the field between the 20-yard line and the goal line. When you watch football on television in these days of video technology, the producers of the game will sometimes "paint" a red line across the 20-yardline to mark this area of the field. How does the "red zone" change the game? The field is shorter. Receivers don't have as far to run. Both the offense and defense are compressed. For the team with the ball, it is a time to exercise care not to fumble, thus blowing a chance for a touchdown or a field goal and losing all the ground the team had gained to be in the "red zone."

From a financial planning point of view, the "red zone" is when you are within five to 10 years of retirement. Decisions you make then are crucial. Why? Because time is compressed. You may not have the time to make up for losses in the stock market you had in your younger years. You save more diligently and invest more conservatively, knowing you will soon be severing your umbilical paycheck and living off your savings and investments.

This is also a time when a miscalculation can be devastating.

One of history's bravest pilots was Amelia Earhart. She disappeared in 1937 attempting to become the first woman to fly around the world. She was an intelligent woman who never backed away from a challenge. Five years to the day after Charles Lindbergh flew across the Atlantic in the Spirit of Saint Louis, Amelia took to the skies to become the first woman to do it. Today, a trans-Atlantic flight is no big deal. But in those days, it took immense courage. Three women died trying to set that record.

Amelia was always trying something new. She flew her first airplane at the age of 23. Piloting a used biplane, she set her first record by flying to an altitude of 14,000 feet, a feat that remained unduplicated for many years. When she became famous, and the spotlight began to focus on her personal life, she friskily told reporters that her marriage to author, publisher and explorer George Putnam was a "partnership" with "dual control," an obvious aviation reference.

Victim of a Miscalculation

On June 1, 1937, at 10 a.m., the twin engines of Amelia Earhart's newly rebuilt Lockheed 10 Electra airplane thundered to life as she began the last aviation challenge she would ever undertake. The plane left Miami and began the 29,000-mile island-hopping trip around the world. She landed in New Guinea with 7,000 miles to go on June 29. Historians think the miscalculations that would cost Amelia her life were due in part to inaccurate maps. Amelia's navigator had calculated, with the huge expanse of the Pacific Ocean before them, their next "hop" would be a small speck in the ocean named Howland Island, 2,556 miles away. If the course were off by the width of a hair, they would miss it.

The next miscalculation may have been fuel. Every unessential item was removed from the plane to take on more fuel. Amelia and others had miscalculated the weather, too. Weather forecasting was an inexact science in those days. Clear skies were predicted, but Amelia flew her plane into overcast skies and rain showers. Her last radio transmissions were faint, reporting that she was in cloudy weather, flying at 1,000 feet, looking for the island and running out of fuel.

Few would disagree Amelia Earhart's fate was the result of several miscalculations.[29]

Money Miscalculations

Feeling financially secure as we approach retirement requires that we are careful and that our calculations are spot on. Calculations are math. One of the most crucial calculations is how much money you need to save before you can safely retire.

I am usually no big fan of TV commercials, but one that caught my attention some time ago was produced by a large insurance company that asked a sampling of people to estimate how much they would need have saved in order to retire and maintain a comfortable lifestyle the rest of their lives. Nearly everyone polled grossly underestimated the amount. The way the commercial illustrated the point was clever.

The narrator says, "We asked people how much money they think they will need when they retire." The participants get to choose a ribbon with an amount of money written on one end, and pull the ribbon until it runs out. The higher the amount on the ribbon, the more years of retirement are funded. The camera then records the reactions of the participants when their ribbons run out after five or 10 years of retirement because they chose a low number. A young man in his 20s guesses just enough to get

[29] History. "Amelia Earhart." http://www.history.com/topics/amelia-earhart.

him to age 70 and comically tries to stretch the ribbon by tugging on it. A middle-aged woman shakes her head regretfully when her ribbon runs out at 75.

Another commercial has a man walking his dog down a tree-lined street. Under the man's arm is a very large number representing the amount he has calculated he needs to have save for retirement. He encounters a neighbor standing on a ladder trimming hedges. The number under the dog-walker's arm is obscured by the camera angle, but it is specific — something like $1,250,000. Sitting atop the hedge is the nebulous word, "Gazillion."

The hedge trimmer asks the dog walker, "Wha'cha got there?"

"It's my retirement number," he replies. "It's the amount of money I need to have saved up before I can safely retire."

Then he asks the hedge trimmer, "Is that your number?" and points to the big word "Gazillion" on top of the hedge.

"Yeah, gazillion, bazillion. I'm just going to throw something at it and hope it's enough," the hedge trimmer responds.

What's the point? The man on the ladder hadn't done any planning. He was clueless in his calculations as to specifically how much money he would need for retirement.

Suppose you want to retire in 10 years. If you can tell a competent financial advisor how much income you want, then the advisor should be able to tell you specifically how much you will need to put away each month or each year to get you there. Then you can make the correct calculations and reach your "landing zone."

The most critical piece of the retirement puzzle for most folks is income. What do you want your paycheck to be once you retire, and how long will it last?

For most people, arriving at these calculations is a product of (a) analysis, and (b) decision-making. I have had a few people come to my office who have saved so little for retirement that I could not help them. What is worse is when they have accumulated so much debt that they must first dig out of a deep hole before they can even begin. Unfortunately for them, unless they become the beneficiary of some kind of financial windfall, like an inheritance or winning a lottery, they will have to adjust their lifestyle dramatically or work longer than they intended. That's the only way to make it work.

On the other hand, some with whom I consult are pleasantly surprised to learn that, when they measure the amount they have saved against their budget, their goals, legacy expectations and expenses, they could have retired years ago and just didn't know it! I find most people don't plan to fail, they just fail to plan!

Miscalculating Your Risk Tolerance

How do you calculate risk tolerance? Isn't it just a feeling? A notion of how much you can stand to lose before you pull the plug on an investment? During America's financial crisis of 2008, stock market prices tumbled 57 percent from their peak in October 2007 to their bottom in March 2009. Lives of many retirees and pre-retirees were changed forever. Balances in retirement accounts lost a staggering $2.8 trillion. Those are just numbers on a page until we consider them in human terms.

A New York Times article entitled, "After the Storm, the Little Nest Eggs That Couldn't" put it in perspective:

> "...many Americans lost tens of thousands, even hundreds of thousands of dollars, when the markets and their 401(k)s swooned in 2008 — all told, 401(k) plans and individual retirement accounts lost $2.8 trillion in value. Thirty-six percent of American workers age 55 to 64 say they have less than

$25,000 in retirement savings, according to a survey by the Employee Benefit Research Institute."[30]

The article went on to relate individual stories of real people whose financial lives were turned upside down, and their plans for retirement wrecked.

When I speak at seminars, I am amazed at how the mood of the audience can change from one group to another. Sometimes world events can trigger these attitude shifts. If the world event in question involves a negative impact on the economic climate, you can feel the tension and see the worry on the faces of the crowd. One of the most memorable events like this occurred on Oct. 29, 2008, when the Dow dropped 777.68 points in a single day. It was the steepest and deepest nosedive Wall Street had ever experienced. People were in shock, and I happened to be conducting a seminar a few days afterward.

"What in blue blazes is going on?" A man asked me. "How did this happen? Surely someone should have seen this coming!" As it turned out, the man had lost thousands of dollars and would lose even more before the economic nightmare was over. Making matters worse, he and his wife were only weeks away from their planned retirement date, and they had no idea how they would replace the money.

I had a prepared presentation, but I put it on hold and just opened the meeting up for questions. What this stunned group mostly wanted to know was what had caused the economic crash. At that time, I didn't know — not entirely anyway. No one did. Later, we would learn mega banks deemed "too big to fail" had put too much of their assets on the line with mortgage-backed securities, and that bad loans had caused the financial house of cards to start collapsing. But the real culprit for so many

---

[30] Steven Green. New York Times. March 8, 2012. "After the Storm, the Little Nest Eggs that Couldn't." http://www.nytimes.com/2012/03/08/business/retire-mentspecial/recovering-from-a-crash-to-make-a-second-act.html.

having lost so much of their wealth virtually overnight was these investors miscalculating just how risky the stock market could be for life's savings.

A woman near the front asked, "Why didn't anyone warn us something like this could happen?" It was a reasonable question, and I wanted to give an answer that wouldn't offend, but it was difficult. I have a tendency to not mince words when discussing serious topics.

"That's a good question, ma'am," I said. "I would pose that question to those who encouraged you to keep so much of your assets in the stock market when you were only months away from retirement."

Then, I softened the answer by explaining there is a measure of risk in everything we do.

"You will assume a measure of risk when you drive home from this meeting," I said. "The problem arises when we take on too much risk, like by driving on roads when conditions are unsafe or ignoring traffic laws or stop lights. I used the example of physical risk. When we were younger, we thought nothing of jumping and running, playing contact sports. As we age, however, our bodies send us signals that we should be more cautious. Ignoring those signals can cause us harm."

"It's the same with investing," I continued. "The older we are, the closer we are to retirement, the more careful we should be with our life's savings."

Most heads nodded in agreement at this, but I knew there were many who had lost large chunks of their retirement savings and were wondering what they could do right then to get it back. The knee-jerk reaction, and the advice some who are not legitimate retirement income planners might give, might have been to go back to the same roulette wheel and go "double-or-nothing," as they say in Las Vegas. But that would have been a major miscalculation for someone approaching retirement. No one in that room knew how long it would take for the market to recover what had been lost, but it would take 5 ½ years for the stock market to climb back to where it was before the crash.

The Associated Press, in an article that appeared on March 5, 2013, proclaimed, "The stock market is back," after the Dow Jones Industrial Average crested the apex from which it tumbled in 2008. But that was not quite true, was it — especially not for someone in retirement who had to deplete a dwindling, nonrenewable resource to pay bills and maintain lifestyle? Also lost was the opportunity for return on investment.[31]

Hindsight being 20/20, of course, the best course of action would have been to have protected one's assets *before* the crash by making more conservative investment decisions. That ship had sailed, of course. The best option now was to preserve what assets were left, get the best return possible without losing any more, and do some serious planning for retirement income that would last.

I knew many in that room back in 2008 would probably end up postponing their retirement at least for a few years. Others would pare down their lifestyles and become more conservative in their spending. Still others would forfeit a portion of the legacy they had intended to leave their heirs. Perhaps they would get one of those bumper stickers that say, "We Are Spending Our Children's Inheritance." None of those options were good, I knew, but miscalculation comes with consequences.

Take Action

Have you ever wondered why deer suddenly freeze when they find themselves caught in the headlights of an oncoming

---

[31] Associated Press. March 3, 2013. "Dow hits new record, regaining losses from Great Recession." http://www.nj.com/business/in-dex.ssf/2013/03/dow_hits_new_record_regaining.html.

car? It's as if they know they may be moments away from danger, but they can't move. Biologist David Yancy explains deer are most active around sunrise and sunset, and that their vision is perfect for low light. "A deer's eyesight is crepuscular (derived from the Latin word for "twilight")," he says. "When a headlight beam hits the deer's fully-dilated eyes, they are momentarily blind. They don't know what to do, so they do nothing at all."

People are that way with money decisions sometimes. They don't know what to do, so they do nothing. Financial decisions can be complex, true. But to go back to the medical metaphors, postponing necessary medical treatment because it is a little complex to comprehend or involves a measure of trust can be hazardous to your health. Postponing planning for one's financial future can be hazardous to your wealth.

Once you have done your due diligence, checked out the credentials of your financial advisor, interviewed them thoroughly, and checked out that he or she is trustworthy, then by all means take positive action for your financial future.

About the Author

Mark A. Lloyd, CEP®, RFC, is the principal owner of The Lloyd Group, Inc. He is a Certified Estate Planner and a Registered Financial Consultant. Lloyd is the host of the nationally syndicated "Financial Symphony" radio and television show, and author of "Protect Yourself and Those You Love: Estate Planning Essentials." He is a popular speaker at estate planning and retirement seminars and believes strongly in educating his clients and the community. As an Investment Advisor Representative and insurance professional, Mark has qualified for and received some of the most highly respected designations offered in the financial advisory community. He has been developing comprehensive retirement plans and estate plans for more than 25 years.

Mark was born and raised in Delaware, but since 1990 has called Suwanee, Georgia, a suburb of Atlanta, home. His first job was working for a chemical company selling hand soap and mineral spirits. In 1990, he decided to follow his older brother, Benjie, into the insurance industry. Soon he was the top agent for a life insurance company. In 1996, he founded the Lloyd Group, a financial advisory firm that currently has more than $140 million under management.

Music has played an important role in Mark's life.

"When I was a kid, my father drove me to piano lessons every Monday," remembers Mark. "I learned to play drums in middle school. By the time I graduated from high school, I was in Nashville, Tennessee, playing music professionally."

Mark still loves playing music, but now only plays at the church he attends in Atlanta.

Mark is married to the former Michelle Osman.

Acknowledgments

I would like to express my gratitude to the many people who saw me through this project and to all those who provided support to me through the many conversations and brainstorming sessions that ultimately helped me shape my observations and opinions for this book.

I appreciate the many individuals who I've met these last 27 years who helped create the stories I was able to share to make this valuable information easier to understand. All of you, my clients, have made a difference in my life and you're the reason why I am passionate in helping as many folks as I can. This gives me a true purpose in my life and I am forever grateful. Thank you for the trust and faith you have given us all these years.

I would be remiss if I did not mention Advisors Excel and the important role they have played in our success, introducing us to other advisors and sharing their ideas. They have given us so many ideas and tools to use that it's impossible not to achieve success with so much available at our fingertips. I would especially like to thank my editor, Tom Bowen, for helping me focus my prose and get the book from my mind into print and ready for publishing.

I have to thank my staff. Heidi Lennon, our VP of operations and marketing, is my right hand and left hand, taking great care of my clients and staff as well as helping me stay focused on helping as many families that I can. Blake, Drew, Cliff and Creston, our advisors, thank you for all you do caring for our clients and sharing your knowledge to many families every day. Mark Jr., my oldest son, and Allison, my youngest daughter, you bless me by allowing me to be a part of your life daily by being a part of the firm and I know you know, but I love you both. The rest of my staff that makes the Lloyd Group tick, thank you from the bottom of my heart. There are too many to mention, but you are in our thoughts every day. My endeavor was to provide some surefire planning to enable retirees to not outlive their money, and it is my sincere hope that this book accomplishes this.

Above all, I wish to express my eternal gratitude to my wife, Michelle, whose patience during this journey was inexhaustible and whose contribution to this project was invaluable. Our 28-year marriage has been a wonderful experience for me, and this is largely due to her unfailing support. She knows I love her, but it seems appropriate to say that out loud here. She also recognizes my second love is helping families achieve their life goals. I will always be grateful for the support and encouragement the rest of my family gave me in this endeavor, in spite of the time it took away from them. Ashley, Mandy and Andrew and all the grandbabies, I love you very much. Thank you to my parents, Ben and Anna Lloyd. You inspire me every day to be a better son, husband, father and Pop-Pop.